# It Takes More Than Good Looks

*Nobody—NOBODY—marries words and pictures like Wayne Freedman. I've been inspired by him and stolen from him. "Television journalism" is not an oxymoron in his hands, but his greatest gift may be as a teacher of storytelling. If you aspire to excellence, you ought to know what he knows.*
    Ray Farkas, Independent News and Documentary Producer

*Wayne Freedman is commonly called the best local television feature reporter in America, but he's much more than that. Wayne understands how to find—and tell—the essence of every story. Anyone who's interested in reporting and really connecting with viewers should read this book.*
    Bob Papper, Professor of Telecommunications, Ball State University
    Author, *Broadcast News Writing Stylebook*

*Wayne Freedman reminds us that, above all, we are storytellers. He takes us back to the basics and reminds us that the story is not always the one your news director or producer wanted you to do. He urges us to remember that in these highly competitive times, you must take risks to excel. In this book, he shares his keen eye and love of words to create an incredible learning experience for anyone who's in the business of broadcast journalism.*
    Mary Ellen Geist, KGO Radio/ABC News, San Francisco

*If you read only a few chapters, and let only a fraction of Freedman's wisdom sink in, you'll learn the difference between reporting a story, and telling one.*
    Stephanie Riggs, Emmy Award–Winning Anchor/Reporter, KCNC-TV, Denver

*A serious book, but deceptively so, like a smuggler. A fun read with some important learning within. If this were a book of magic, they'd throw him out of the fraternity for giving away the secrets.*
    Ron Brown, Anchor/Reporter, WGEM-TV

*Inspiring and educational, but also fun reading. I took it on vacation and couldn't put it down, even at the beach.*
    Karen O'Leary, Reporter, KIRO-TV

*For nigh on to twenty years, I've said Wayne Freedman "makes the best television" of anybody working in news in this country. Sometimes irreverent, usually witty, and always insightful with his storytelling, Wayne's at his best when he's looking at the ripples emanating from the spot story everyone else sees. If you want to succeed in this business, you should learn about the world, hone your basic skills, then dedicate yourself to such versatility and craftsmanship as Wayne Freedman displays every time he goes out on a story.*
    Mackie Morris, Journalist, Educator, and Consultant

# It Takes More
## Than Good Looks . . .

# It Takes More
# Than Good Looks . . .

*To Succeed at Television*
*News Reporting*

WAYNE FREEDMAN

BONUS BOOKS
Chicago and Los Angeles

07  06  05  04  03                                                    5  4  3  2  1

Library of Congress Cataloging-in-Publication Data

Freedman, Wayne.
  It takes more than good looks—to succeed at television news
reporting / Wayne Freedman.
     p.  cm.
Includes index.
  ISBN 1-56625-188-5
  1. Television broadcasting of news. I. title.


PN4784.T4F74 2003
070.1′95—dc21

                                              2003004232


Bonus Books
875 N. Michigan Ave., Ste. 1416
Chicago, IL 60611

*Printed in the United States of America*

*To Susan and Lauren*

*For my parents, Mike and Alicia*

*And to the old schoolers, wherever you are. Pass it on.*

# Contents

## Part I: Fundamentals

| | | |
|---|---|---|
| 1. | Pursuit | 3 |
| 2. | Find a Person; Tell a Story | 13 |
| 3. | Questions and Answers: Interviewing for Sound Bites | 37 |
| 4. | Narrative Structure: Beginnings, Middles, Endings, and Timelines | 63 |

## Part II: Pragmatics

| | | |
|---|---|---|
| 5. | The Facts of Life in Television News | 87 |
| 6. | Getting Ahead: Create Your Own Luck | 99 |
| 7. | When You Have No Time: Hamburger Helpers for Television News | 117 |
| 8. | Thread Stories Around Spontaneous Moments | 131 |
| 9. | Using Comparison, Contrast, and Opposites as Storytelling Devices | 139 |
| 10. | Stand-Ups | 151 |
| 11. | Face Time: Going Live | 165 |
| 12. | We Interrupt This Serious Book . . . | 179 |
| 13. | Keep It Simple: The Suitcase Theory of Packaging | 183 |
| 14. | Report What You Find: *What Is* Will Always Be More Interesting Than What You Make Up | 187 |

## Part Three: Philosophy

15. Craftsmanship and Restraint: Don't Mess with the Pope        199
16. A Few Thoughts About Writing                                 205
17. Seek the Simple Truths                                       217
18. Look Beyond the Superficial: Sometimes,
       Stories Can Be About Something Else                       233
19. Finding Stories: Just Ask, Look, Listen, and Think           247
20. One Story, Start to Finish                                   261
21. Change the Small Worlds First                                277

*Acknowledgments*                                                283
*Index*                                                          287

Part I

# FUNDAMENTALS

# 1

## Pursuit

When television news people look at clocks, they invariably wish the hands would move slower, not faster. If you're a reporter, you may have days, hours, minutes, or seconds to finish a story. It doesn't matter. You're always aware of time's relentless forward march. You can't help feeling hurried, and sometimes worried.

For television news crews, every day brings a new challenge. Some of those days are more trying than others, none more so than a Wednesday in June 2000. KGO-TV photographer Doug Laughlin and I had gone to Pebble Beach, California, for general news coverage of the U.S. Open golf tournament. Our troubles began early, when a security man stopped us near the first tee.

"That is only a press pass," he said with authority. "Your press pass is not a photo pass. You need a photo pass to take that camera on the course."

"Where do we get a photo pass?"

"You can't get a photo pass, " he said indifferently.

"But we need a photo pass."

"Everybody needs a photo pass."

Clearly, this man had perfected something in life—his imitation of a brick wall. We'd planned to do a story about watching golf from the gallery, but he cared only about rules and technicalities. "Your press pass grants access to the press tent, but nowhere else," he droned with the charm of a customs agent. "See here. Your press pass does not say 'photo.'"

Consider our predicament. I'd begged for this assignment and promised to deliver one quality piece every day. Now, with a deadline approaching, we'd lost our story.

"Now what?" I asked of no one in particular. If you work in this business, you've probably asked that question, too. Angst comes with the job, and I felt buried beneath a mountain of it. "What do we do now?"

As if in answer to our question, a golf cart pulled up and stopped a few feet away. Two tournament officials climbed out. One of them carried a clipboard, on top of which sat a small but ornate piece of silver. It looked familiar—very familiar. Doug caught my nod, grabbed his camera, and rolled tape as we approached.

"Excuse me," I asked, "but isn't that . . . ?"

"It is, indeed," the driver boasted. "This is the lid to the U.S. Open trophy."

But he held only the lid, mind you, disembodied from its much larger cup. "Where's the rest?"

"Back in its carrying case," said the man, who identified himself as Rand Jerris, a librarian for the United States Golf Association. "We're taking the lid in for repairs."

"You mean the trophy is broken?"

"Of course it's not broken. We certainly have all the parts for it. We're just going to go for a quick fix." Jerris appeared to be enjoying his moment in front of the lens. He handed me the lid, which featured a winged, female victory figure on top, but one of those wings was missing. Then he dangled a clear plastic sandwich bag. Inside—the wing. Jerris had done everything but pack that severed appendage in ice.

Clearly we'd struck, if not gold, then silver. The U.S. Open trophy, the holy icon of American golf, was maimed, cracked, ravaged, plundered, abused, or something. Better yet for our purposes, the USGA would be taking it to a place beyond the hoopla and the press passes. Someone, somewhere would be fixing it, and that could make a good story. "So who's doing the work for you?" I asked innocently.

"We're not sure, yet. There have to be some silversmiths in town," Jerris speculated. "We'll try one of them."

"Mind if we go along?"

Rand Jerris, the mild-mannered, bookish USGA historian, looked at us as if we were insane. "Why would you care about that? But I'll check."

Jerris entered the press tent to consult his superiors. Doug and I didn't want to appear overeager, so we waited just outside, peeking in. Five minutes passed, then ten. No word.

Jerris showed the lid to his boss, who then looked over at us. I smiled benignly. He scowled back.

All the while, countless other reporters sauntered past, their heads buried in scoring sheets. They glanced at the pairings board and spoke into mobile telephones, but none seemed to notice the broken lid of the U.S. Open trophy. How could no one else be curious?

After fifteen minutes, I gave in to impatience and approached Jerris and his boss, who gave me a disdainful once-over. "We at the USGA don't believe this would be conducive to a positive image of the Open," he said dismissively. "We won't help."

"But how did the trophy break?"

"It just did," he replied.

"Who broke it? And when?"

"Now, really," he tut-tutted. "This is an internal matter."

"Come on," I persisted. "It's a good human interest angle."

"Not to us," he said icily.

The official seemed determined to act like a jerk, so I played along. "You know, we already have pictures of the lid on video tape," I said, and then paused for effect. "It's all we need for a story. But here's a deal. Give us a photo pass with full access to the course for the next four days, and we'll be happy to hold this."

"Nice try," huffed the boss. He marched off without even saying goodbye. Maybe he thought we were bluffing—and we certainly would have kept our part of the offer—but I was partly relieved. The man had been so snootily rude that he'd made this into a contest between us and them. Besides, the trophy was a better story.

## Find Small Stories in the Big Ones, and Big Stories in the Small Ones

At heart, I'm just like anybody else who enjoys telling stories. But, as someone who does it for a living, I must deal with the added element of competition. Most reporters feel the same pressure. To survive and excel, we're constantly searching for novel angles, and developing our own methods of finding them. Mine is to keep an eye on other reporters and, when possible, to work in an opposite direction. Note what they're getting, and also what they're missing.

My philosophy is that, in every story, large or small, we should tell the news of the day. Taken at face value, that news is often fairly forgettable. But, by looking deeper into those everyday stories, you may find something simple, approachable, or telling about the world in which we live. That's my joy in this business—finding stories within stories. There are big stories in the small ones, and small stories in the big ones. They reveal the universal truths about life.

I'll take a story like that, anytime. Viewers tend to remember and appreciate them.

Back in the press tent, Doug and I knew we had such a segment within reach, but we'd have to find the person fixing that trophy. If the United States Golf Association didn't want to cooperate, so be it. "Let's get the story without them," I told Doug.

We returned to town, had a couple of coffees, and then opened the Yellow Pages. For the entire area, they listed only one silversmith, Colonial Silver.

I gave Jerris about a one-hour head start and then called the number. "Hello?" answered a pleasant man with an Italian accent. I identified myself, and realized the next line would be crucial. To sound uncertain would have given us away. "Are you the man who is single-handedly saving the U.S. Open?" I asked in a congratulatory manner.

Silence.

I dropped a name. "Has Rand Jerris come by with the trophy yet?"

"The trophy's right here." He told us his name was Carmelo Tringali, and said he owned the place.

It felt like progress, but I still had to be careful. To establish some semblance of credibility, I rambled casually about the few facts we knew. Remember, we'd held the lid and seen the broken wing. Jerris told us he was taking it for repairs. That was true. At just the right moment, I made my pitch, "Mr. Tringali, we want to do a report about the man repairing the trophy."

"What about the golf people?" he asked.

"The USGA knows we want to do this story." We hadn't lied, and Mr. Tringali left it at that, thankfully. He invited us over.

In person, Carmelo Tringali is a gentle, soft-spoken man with black glasses, a gray beard, and a tarnish-stained apron. Doug put a microphone on him and quickly set some lights. Mr. Tringali led us to the back of his shop, where, on a table piled with damaged heirlooms, he unceremoniously lifted a soiled piece of denim, revealing the lid.

"What did they tell you when they came in?" I asked.

"They said, 'See if you can fix this broken thing.'"

"Thing." Mr. Tringali, who did not play golf and knew little if any of the trophy's tradition, called it a "thing." "To me, this is just a piece of silver," he said with a chuckle. "It's just another broken lid." He saw no difference between the U.S. Open trophy and grandma's tea service, or Billy's first trumpet, or any of the other golf trophies at which he pointed. "I fixed those, too."

What a change in fortune. We'd begun the morning in desperation, but the fun of being a television news reporter is that, on any given day, you never know what you're going to find, where you're going to go, or whom you're going to meet. Every new assignment is a learning experience. While this one wasn't typical, it exemplifies several of the themes and survival skills in this book:

1. Never give up.
2. Recognize opportunities.
3. Be willing to change plans at a moment's notice.
4. If you identify a main character, you can always tell a story.
5. Layer your story. Speak to viewers at several factual and emotional levels.

6. A piece doesn't need to change the world to be memorable. Small stories can make just as big an impression.

Our trophy piece certainly fit those criteria. Carmelo Tringali made a wonderful contrast to the USGA's pretentious pomp. This humble, unassuming craftsman would leave his mark on a crown jewel of golf and, in a competitive journalistic environment, nobody else found the story.

Back at his shop, Mr. Tringali clamped the broken wing before torching it into place. Our story needed an ending. He still wore a microphone as I observed off-handedly, "Mr. Tringali, did you ever consider how the entire golfing world will see your work, but never know your name."

"That's okay. I'll try to do a good job," he said intently. "When do they need this thing, again? Sunday?"

Yes. Of course. Sunday. And, on that day, with millions watching, Tiger Woods hoisted the very same U.S. Open trophy. He would follow that victory with others at the British Open, the PGA Championship, and then the Masters—four consecutive majors.

No one knew it at the time, but that U.S. Open trophy became the first of what some writers called the Grand Slam, and others, the Tiger Slam. By any measure, it made golf history.

Imagine—four trophies on Tiger Woods's mantle, and, if you'd looked closely, you'd have seen that one of them had a welded wing.

## TIGER'S TROPHY
### June 2000

[TRACK]
(see players practicing)
AMONG THE POSSIBLE HEROES AT THIS YEAR'S U.S.
OPEN, HERE'S A NAME YOU HAVEN'T HEARD—
CARMELO TRINGALI.

[SOT]

Tringali: "I'm just a lucky person, I guess."

[TRACK]

WE WOULD NEVER HAVE MET HIM, IF NOT FOR
TWO USGA OFFICIALS WHO TOOK A RIDE IN A GOLF
CART WITH A PIECE OF SILVER IN THEIR HANDS. BUT
WAIT . . .

[SOT]

(file tape: crowd cheers as a champion holds the
trophy in triumph)

[TRACK]

(shots of trophy and lid)
DOESN'T THAT PIECE LOOK A LITTLE LIKE THIS?
COULD IT BE?

[SOT]

Rand Jerris: "This is the lid to the U.S. Open
trophy."

[TRACK]

JUST THE LID, MIND YOU, DISEMBODIED FROM THE
CUP. AND, IF YOU LOOK CLOSELY, NOTE THE WING,
BROKEN OFF FROM THE VICTORY FIGURE. THEY
WRAPPED IT IN PLASTIC, LIKE A SEVERED LIMB.

[SOT]

Wayne: "YOU MEAN THE TROPHY IS BROKEN?"

Jerris: "Of course it's not broken. We certainly have
all the parts for it. We're just going to go for a
quick fix."

[WAYNE STAND-UP]
AND THAT IS ALL THEY WOULD SAY. IN FACT, THE
MORE WE QUESTIONED USGA OFFICIALS, THE LESS
THEY WOULD TELL US. NOT HOW THE CUP BROKE.
OR BY WHOM. OR WHEN. "NO BIG DEAL," THEY
KEPT INSISTING. "ACCIDENTS HAPPEN."

[TRACK]
(exterior, the Colonial Silver)
AND ACCIDENTS GET FIXED. BUT, FOR NEARBY
PACIFIC GROVE, THE YELLOW PAGES LIST ONLY ONE
SILVERSMITH.

[SOT]
Wayne to Tringali: "WHAT DID THEY TELL YOU WHEN
THEY CAME IN?"

Tringali: "They said, 'See if you can fix this broken
thing.'"

Wayne: "THING?"

Tringali: "Yeah. Thing."

[WAYNE TRACK]
THIS THING. ALSO KNOWN AS THE HOLY GRAIL OF
AMERICAN GOLF. THIS THING, WHICH HAS PASSED
FROM HAND TO HAND OF GOLFING LEGENDS,
LIVING AND DEAD, FOR A HUNDRED AND FIVE
YEARS. PAYNE STEWART . . . JACK NICKLAUS . . .

[SOT]
Wayne to Tringali: "BEN HOGAN HAD THIS TROPHY."

Tringali: "Ben Hogan? Never heard of him."

[TRACK]
CARMELO TRINGALI NEVER HEARD OF MOST OF
THEM, AND, UNTIL TODAY, NEVER KNEW THIS
TROPHY EXISTED. BUT FIXING IT SHOULDN'T BE A
PROBLEM, HE SAYS.

[SOT]
Tringali: "To me, this is just a piece of silver. It's
just another broken lid."

[TRACK]
. . . NO DIFFERENT FROM GRANDMA'S TEA SERVICE,
OR ANY OTHER GOLF TROPHY . . .
(file of victorious golfers)
EXCEPT THAT THIS ONE MEANS A LITTLE MORE.
AND NOW CARMELO TRINGALI CAN CLAIM A PIECE
OF THE CUP'S ILLUSTRIOUS HISTORY. MAYBE IT'S
BEST THAT HE DOESN'T KNOW.

[SOT]
Wayne to Tringali: "MR. TRINGALI, DID YOU EVER
CONSIDER HOW THE ENTIRE GOLFING WORLD WILL
SEE YOUR WORK, BUT NEVER KNOW YOUR NAME?"

Tringali: "I'll try to do a good job."

[TRACK]
HE SAYS HE'LL HAVE IT READY BY SUNDAY.

# 2

---

# Find a Person; Tell a Story

---

Most people watch television news the same way they pass an automobile accident. They gawk, assess the damage, drive on, and, within two minutes, forget about it. What's to remember? Cars, a few bent fenders. They don't know the people involved, so they don't have a direct interest, so why dwell on it?

But their indifference would disappear if they recognized a car in the wreck as belonging to a friend or neighbor. Then, they might stop or try to help, and they'd certainly think about that accident for longer than two minutes.

Television news stories are not car wrecks, of course, but the comparison works because many reporters approach them the same way. They present facts, but fail to make them relevant or meaningful to the viewers passing by.

In a perfect world, every news story would directly affect everyone. In practice, this doesn't often happen, but good reporters find ways to make the material compelling, anyway. They recognize that, in its purest form, television news can and should make people experience something—anger, fear, wonder, laughter, sadness. In most daily news stories, the road to a viewer's head travels through the gut. Television is a visceral medium. People remember what they feel. If you reach a person on that level, you'll get all of him.

## Use Characters to Tell Stories

But reporters often fall short of that goal. Sometimes I wonder why we call our work television news "stories" when so many of us overlook the "story" part. We get distracted by deadlines and details, and forget a fundamental: *stories have characters.*

It's so simple. Events happen to people. When you build stories around them, audiences take a stake in those people and their situations. Let viewers see a little of themselves, or someone they know. By using characters, reporters can ground any story in the real world.

### Joey

Not long ago we covered a highway closure in a snowstorm. The producer asked for a live shot wrapped around a ninety-second package, so we stopped at a checkpoint where drivers either installed tire chains or paid people to do the job for them. Reporters have taken that angle countless times, but then we spotted a young man crouching in the snow next to a car, and he gave the story a different twist. His name was Joey Cattrell, and he'd been riding in the small sedan with five friends, any of whom would have happily split the cost of a chain installer. But that didn't sit right with Joey, who asked, "Why waste money?"

Joey Cattrell is the kind of person you might call a "doer." Everybody knows someone like him. As our camera watched, he removed his parka, rolled around on his back in the dirty, frozen muck, and attached those chains by himself. By interviewing Joey, watching his friends stand around, and developing them all as characters, we made the story of that that traffic jam a little more approachable, because we found a universal truth:

> [TRACK]
> AT A TIME LIKE THIS, IT'S ALWAYS NICE TO HAVE A
> GUY LIKE JOEY CATTRELL AROUND.

## The Formula

Joey provides a good example of a simple and reliable journalistic formula. *Find a person. Tell a story. Weave the facts of the news inside of it.* See news events as daily dramas, and the people within them as role-players. When you look beyond a newsmaker's function and examine the individual instead, you can make almost anyone interesting, from an embattled politician to an overworked detective, to a man on the street, to a civil engineer with a clipboard.

## The Math Wiz

In 2002 the Port of Oakland, California, purchased four monstrous cargo cranes from a company in Japan, which then sent them across the Pacific Ocean aboard an ungainly looking, top-heavy ship. Those cranes towered above the water, and couldn't have been built any taller. Having traveled several thousand miles, they would pass beneath the San Francisco/Oakland Bay Bridge with only twenty-six inches of clearance.

The port knew that number because it employed an engineer who had done the calculations. The day before those cranes arrived, we tracked him down for a story. During the interview he showed us the math and, after seeing it, I asked if he had done well in his SAT college entrance exam.

"Perfect score," boasted the engineer. That small fact made the story, and turned a public servant into a regular guy. Any viewer who ever struggled with a math problem could relate to him. It also gave the piece an opening line:

> [SOT]
> (pencil scratches paper as the engineer calculates aloud)
>
> [TRACK]
> IF YOU EVER WONDERED WHO GETS A PERFECT MATH SCORE IN HIS SAT, HERE IS YOUR ANSWER. AND ON A DAY LIKE TOMORROW, BE GLAD HE DID.

## Interviews as Salesmanship: The Unemployment Line

At times, however, it won't be practical to do a story about just one person. If the story concerns a larger issue, you may need to tell it from several points of view.

In July of 1991, CBS News made cost cuts, and I was one of them. Such misfortune happens to almost everyone in this business, eventually. Don't take it personally. Four months later, I went to work for KGO-TV in San Francisco, beginning as a freelance reporter.

Fittingly, in that first week the producers asked me to do a story about California's unemployment rate reaching double digits. Our desk had already set up an interview with a state official who would interpret the numbers.

No, it wasn't the most human angle, but a reporter should never argue with his employer when, technically, he's still an employment statistic himself. Photographer Pam Partee and I followed instructions, went to the bureaucrat's office, and tried to keep our eyes open during the interview.

Surely, though, there had to be a better way to approach the assignment. I called the desk. "What if we go to an unemployment office and interview the people waiting there?" Just two weeks earlier I had stood in such a line, and I remembered how we'd commiserated with one another. If Pam and I could capture some of that for the news, it would give the piece some extra oomph. The desk cleared us to go ahead and try.

In theory, it was a good idea. In practice, the people waiting to make unemployment claims wanted nothing to do with a television crew. "You have to be kidding," said one man.

Clearly, we'd have to do a sales job before conducting any interviews. This isn't unusual. If you report from the field, you already know that, for every person who asks to be on the news, ten others won't want anything to do with you.

This is where the salesmanship comes into play. Asking questions is easy, but it takes work to find the right people and convince them to talk. We ask for their time. We ask for their honesty. Adding to our difficulties, we're television news reporters, and many civilians distrust us.

## The Chameleon Theory

When persuading someone to do an interview, follow a proven method of salesmanship. *Let the buyer buy.* In the same way a skilled salesman allows a client to describe his needs before pitching a product, let your subject convince himself that he wants to talk with you. Be honest. Be an active, sympathetic listener. Try to understand his motivations. In persuading people to grant interviews, reporters often become chameleons.

I remember a story in which San Francisco's district attorney made a show of filing charges against an unscrupulous landlord. We tried repeatedly to get that landlord's reaction, but he wouldn't return our calls. Clearly, he didn't want to talk, so we'd have to give him a reason. I called his machine one last time and left the following question: "Do you think the district attorney would make such a big deal of you if he weren't running for re-election? What's your side of the story."

That landlord took the bait and agreed to go on camera. Ultimately, his interview enraged the district attorney even more.

## No Interview Is Worth More Than Your Reputation

Just accept that, no matter how hard you try, you won't make every sale. Don't take it personally. Remain courteous. Keep your dignity. Don't bully, threaten, or follow up with nasty e-mails. Thank the person for listening to your pitch, cut your losses, and move on. Don't hide microphones or surreptitiously roll tape in the hope of stealing a sound bite. Reporters are not in the exploitation business. Respect your subjects as viewers, and your viewers as consumers. Try to keep them on our side. No story is more important than your reputation.

## Sometimes, You Push

But, as we stood in that unemployment office, instinct told me to push with the man who said he didn't want to talk. Although he'd effectively told us to get lost, he pursued the conversation and didn't hold back his feelings. Since he wasn't bashful, I suspected he was mostly worried about what he might say and then be unable to take back. If only we could capture his passion on tape.

"It's my job to convince you to go on camera," I explained to the man. "You can help us, and we can help you. California just reached 10 percent unemployment. We can hear about it from a bureaucrat, or from someone who's living it. Name one person who understands the numbers better than you."

"Why should I trust you?" the man asked.

"Because two weeks ago I was unemployed, and stood in this very same line."

He paused. "It sucks," he finally said. "I'm not a cost-cutting measure. I'm a person. I busted my butt for that company. I gave it four years, and now I'm on the street. They scratched me out like a line item on a balance sheet."

"You need to say that on camera," I suggested. "You know what you're going through, and so do I. But the rest of the world—they may never know unless we tell them." It was, in essence, an offer of complicity; as partners, the two of us would explain the frustrations of unemployment. When he saw my proposal in those terms, the man nodded okay. Pam set the camera and we began.

"What job did you have?" I asked, and then followed with more questions.

"How long did you work there?"

"How long have you been out?"

"Who fired you?"

"How did they do it?"

"What did they say?"

"Did you see it coming?"

The man answered emotionally and, as often happens in such

environments, other people asked to add a few thoughts. Before we left, every person in that unemployment line answered the same series of questions. In the edit room we cut them together, one after another. *Instead of having a dispassionate bureaucrat spout statistics, we built a story with an ensemble cast.* They supplied faces and sentiments to the concept of 10 percent unemployment in California.

## JOBLESS
### July 1991

[TRACK]
IT IS ONE OF THOSE GENERIC GOVERNMENT OFFICES—A LIMBO ZONE, WHERE PEOPLE TAKE NUMBERS AND FILL OUT FORMS USING SHORT LITTLE PENCILS WITH WORN-DOWN ENDS.

[SOT]
Wayne: "WHEN DID THIS HAPPEN?"

Man #1: "About eight months ago."

Man #2: "About nine months."

Man #3: "I was laid off yesterday."

[WAYNE ON CAMERA]
AS AN INSTITUTION, THE UNEMPLOYMENT OFFICE IS A GREAT EQUALIZER. EACH DAY, PEOPLE COME HERE FROM ALL WALKS OF LIFE. AND, IF THEY DIDN'T HAVE ANYTHING IN COMMON BEFORE, THEY DO NOW.

[SOT]
Wayne asks Man #3: "WHAT DID THEY TELL YOU?"

Man #3: "That they were cutting back because the orders were slow and..."

Man #2: "Well the job was deleted and I didn't have any marketable skills . . ."

Man #4: "And then the company downsized. Manufacturing went overseas . . ."

Woman #1: "Yeah, it took ten minutes. I was out."

Man #3: "I gave four years of my can for this job. And they go, 'Goodbye!' They gave all the usual warnings and blah, blah, blah, but I am just booted out on my derriere onto the street."

Wayne asks Man #4: "HAD YOU EVER LAID PEOPLE OFF IN YOUR JOB?"

Man #4: "Yes I had. I laid off sixty-five people at one time. And it wasn't pretty. And it wasn't fun. And now I sort of feel as if I'm being paid back!"

Wayne to Man #2: "HOW MANY JOBS HAVE YOU APPLIED FOR?"

Man #2: "Twenty, maybe twenty-five or thirty . . ."

Man #3: "I go into Joe Smith's store and ask for an application. They look at me like they're giving it to me because they have to, but I know they're thinking they won't hire me. And they're snickering. Hey. I'm just trying to find a job . . ."

Man #4: "In America you are what you do. You can't go anywhere in a social situation, a party, a bar, a golf course. The first question is what's your name and the second is what do you do?"

Woman #1: "You feel as if you don't have as much control over your life as you'd like to, or you're used to."

Man #2: "You feel despondent. You feel anger toward people who are making it. And all you want is the same chance."

[TRACK]
THAT'S ALL ANYONE HERE WANTS . . . A CHANCE, A BREAK, AN END TO UNCERTAINTY. YOU'LL FIND IT IN EVERY CITY AND TOWN IN THE STATE.

Man #2: "I have to keep going. There is a better road somewhere. I know, someday, I'll find it."

[TRACK]
SOMEDAY.
EVEN IF SOMEDAY CAME TODAY, IT WOULDN'T BE SOON ENOUGH.

# Selecting a Principal Character: The Apartment Hunter

Several years ago, low vacancy rates pushed up rental prices for San Francisco apartments. The *San Francisco Chronicle* ran a front-page article, and our producers wanted a piece for that night.

Oh, well. Sometimes, we aren't so much news reporters as news repeaters. Hopefully, when handed a newspaper story, you can find a way to advance or elaborate upon it.

"We'll need the crew back by noon," said our assignment manager. "Seriously, noon. We must have the camera." (I often wonder why we refer to a one-man band as a crew, and people as cameras, but that's the way we do it, no offense intended or taken.) We would have two hours to get out the door, find a story, shoot it, and return.

I saw this as a simple story about supply and demand. We could cover the pertinent facts with two or three lines, probably in a stand-up. To sell it, I thought we should emphasize struggle more than numbers, but, to do so, we needed that personal angle. Where would we find it?

I considered newspaper want ads and apartment complexes, dismissed both, picked up the telephone book, and looked for a rental agency. San Francisco has dozens of them. But which of these places might offer a choice of people who might be good on television?

Then I saw the advertisement for an outfit called Community Rentals in the Castro district, one of San Francisco's more socially diverse neighborhoods. The man who answered the phone said, "Yes, we have clients here." With that, we sealed an unspoken deal. The manager would give us access to people and, in return, we would give him publicity. Half an hour later, we walked through his door and found five apartment hunters.

Again, we faced the same kind of problem as in the unemployment office. Some people just don't like television news crews. They're suspicious. They find the camera intimidating. To get everyone used to us, we interviewed the office manager first. "Everybody wants a perfect apartment," he said with a seen-it-all attitude. "They want to find the Victorian with hardwood floors. And, of course, it's a top unit, lots of light, with a view of the Golden Gate Bridge and the Bay Bridge."

"With an attractive single person living next door?"

"Or beneath them, yes."

Okay. We had one sound bite from a person who could qualify as an expert, and also possibly as a comedian. Next, we needed someone with an apartment challenge. One of the people in that room would become our main character. But who?

It's a quandary reporters face regularly. If they aren't looking specifically for main characters, they're at least trying to find the right people to interview. Every reporter has his own method based on experience.

## Picking People: It's in the Eyes

I found a key to my approach while working as a network page for ABC-TV in Los Angeles. Among our regular assignments, we pages worked a show called *Let's Make a Deal.* It was our job to handle the studio audiences that lined up before tapings. From their numbers, the program would choose a few of the more gregarious to compete on the trading floor where, if they were lucky, host Monty Hall might deal them into a car, a trip to Hawaii, or even a dinette set.

To select the anointed few, *Let's Make a Deal* hired a staff of writer/producers who walked along the line of contestants, most of whom dressed in outlandish costumes. You had to see and hear them to believe it—screaming, teeming masses of adults made up as if for Halloween. They came as teapots, as tennis racquets, as cars, as carrots. One guy came as a corpse. His sign read, "I'm dying for a deal."

As they chose their contestants, those writers took an almost wicked pleasure in working the crowd into a greedy frenzy. Some days, the ordeal lasted fifteen ear-splitting minutes. The writers would pace the line, lean in close to someone, tease, shout, "Who wants a deal?" and then dramatically point a finger: "You!" If we'd been in a church, you might have thought they were healing the sick.

After watching this spectacle for a few weeks, I asked the head writer, "How do you choose someone? How do you know who'll be good?"

That writer looked about fifty, and had worked game shows most of his career. "It's in their eyes," he said, as if disclosing an inside secret. "It's energy. Look for the twinkle in their eyes. If the eyes talk to you, take them."

It was excellent advice. Although choosing people for news stories is not the same as picking game show contestants, some of the same principles apply.

## Audition Your Subjects

So, while scanning the apartment hunters in that rental office, I remembered my writer friend and looked for eye contact, hoping for a twinkle. We moved around the room asking questions, some on camera.

"How long have you been looking?"

"Did you believe it would be this tough?"

"Compare this with something."

"What does 'cottage' mean?"

"How do you define 'quaint'?"

Later, we used several of the answers for quick sound bites. But, more important, these interviews also served as auditions. They helped us discover who spoke well. Who had good energy? Who would the viewers like? With whom could I establish a rapport? Those qualities make a difference because, even in a story as simple as one about high rents, you will, in a limited way, turn your main character into a star.

One woman, Heidi Dubrot, met all the criteria. "What are you doing when you leave here?" I asked.

"Checking out a few apartments."

"Mind if we come along?"

"No problem," she said.

Shortly thereafter, Heidi, my "camera," and I went apartment hunting. Heidi explored one place, then a second, then a third. Through every phase of this dismal search, I asked questions with the camera rolling. That night, our piece presented the straightforward facts of San Francisco's apartment crunch. More important, it made those facts relevant to viewers because they shared Heidi's frustrating search.

Again, a little story about numbers told a bigger one about life.

## HIGH RENTS
### March 1996

[SOT]
(fingers dial phone)


[TRACK]
SHE BEGAN THIS DAY WITH THE BEST INTENTIONS . . .


[SOT]
Heidi talking on phone:
"I'm looking for a two-bedroom in the lower Haight area . . ."

[TRACK]
HEIDI DUBROT DOESN'T WANT THE WORLD. SHE'S SIMPLY GROWN TIRED OF MOOCHING OFF HER PARENTS . . .


[SOT]
(Heidi on the front porch steps of an apartment)

Wayne: "YOU'VE LEFT HOME BEFORE, RIGHT?"

Heidi: "Yes. . . ." (laughs)

[TRACK]
AND SO, THE QUEST . . .

[SOT]
(Heidi on phone, continuing conversation)
"It was already rented?"

[TRACK]
. . . WHICH BEGAT REALITY . . .

[SOT]
(hangs up phone)

[TRACK]
. . . AND LED HER TO THIS DESPERATION CHAMBER,
A PLACE WITH A HOPEFUL NAME . . .

[SOT]
Manager of rental company: "Community Rentals."

[SOT]
Wayne to a client in the rental agency: "IS THIS HELL?"

Woman: "I can't tell, yet."

[TRACK]
(Heidi looks at map)

BY THE TIME THEY GET HERE, MOST APARTMENT
HUNTERS NO LONGER EXPECT TO FIND THE TAJ
MAHAL . . .

[SOT]
Manager: "You know everybody wants a perfect
apartment. They want to find the Victorian with
hardwood floors. And, of course, it's a top unit, lots
of light, with a view of the Golden Gate Bridge and
the Bay Bridge . . ."

Wayne: "WITH AN ATTRACTIVE SINGLE PERSON
LIVING NEXT DOOR?"

Manager: "Or beneath them, yes . . ."

[TRACK]
(behind Heidi as she walks)
AND NOW TO THE SEARCH, BUT WITH TWO-
BEDROOM APARTMENTS AVERAGING TWELVE
HUNDRED DOLLARS IN SAN FRANCISCO, HEIDI
MIGHT HAVE BETTER LUCK TRYING TO FIND THE
GOLDEN FLEECE.

[SOT]
As Heidi talks on a pay telephone, Wayne asks:
"YOU DON'T JUDGE BOOKS BY THEIR COVERS?"

Heidi: "No."

She speaks into phone: "You don't have anything
else available?"

[STAND-UP]
HOW BAD IS IT? WELL, EXPERTS ARE COMPARING
THIS WITH THE NEW YORK APARTMENT CRUNCH OF
THE 1980s. WHY? SUPPLY AND DEMAND, MOSTLY . . .
A ONE PERCENT VACANCY RATE. THE BAY AREA HAS
MORE JOBS THAN EVER. PEOPLE ARE MOVING HERE

TO TAKE THEM. THEY'RE MAKING GOOD MONEY,
BUT NOT ENOUGH MONEY TO BUY REAL ESTATE, SO
RENT PRICES ARE GOING UP.

[SOT]
Wayne to Heidi: "HAVE YOU FIGURED OUT WHAT
SOME OF THE DIFFERENT WORDS MEAN? 'QUAINT,'
FOR EXAMPLE?"

Heidi: "'Quaint' means older."

Wayne: "'COZY' MEANS?"

Heidi: "'Cozy' means small . . ."

[TRACK]
. . . BUT "COTTAGE"—NOW THAT'S A FINE WORD.
AT EIGHT HUNDRED DOLLARS, HEIDI REALLY GOT
HER HOPES UP FOR THIS ONE . . .

[SOT]
(VO Heidi walks)
"Maybe sunny, clean, country-like, that sort of
thing."

[SOT]
(she peeks into the window)
"Oh God . . ." (in disgust)

[TRACK]
SHE FOUND NOBODY HOME, BUT A QUICK PEEK
INSIDE CONFIRMED THAT HANSEL AND GRETEL
NEVER LIVED HERE, AND HEIDI NEVER WILL . . .

[SOT]

Wayne to Heidi: "SO WHAT HAVE WE LEARNED
TODAY?"

Heidi: (laughing) "I've learned I'm going to have to
look some more . . ."

[TRACK]
SITUATIONS WANTED. SINGLE FEMALE, EMPLOYED,
NON-SMOKER, STILL LIVING WITH PARENTS—AND
DESPERATELY SEEKING FREEDOM.

# Not All Characters Are People

Sometimes, your best characters won't even be people, although in
telling their stories you may choose to give them human traits. Try
writing from the perspectives of trees, cars, buildings, storms, fires,
and, of course, animals.

You can't miss with animals. They're innocent. Viewers always
have a soft spot for them, and so do some news managers. I learned
this from a guy named Herb Dudnick, who became my worst
enemy and a great teacher when he assumed the news director's job
at KRON-TV in 1986.

Herb's the man who pioneered late-night network newscasts in
the 1980s. His *NBC News Overnight* broke the mold. It was serious
but casual, and Herb helped maintain that balance by running ani-
mal segments. When Herb came to KRON-TV, our staff already
knew he loved critters, so we assumed the new boss would be warm
and fuzzy. He wasn't. Instead, Herb Dudnick had a brash New York
manner that scared almost everyone.

But the man did have charisma. He showed up looking East
Coast dapper in classy suspenders. Few people in our newsroom

had worn suspenders before, and it's a notable study of newsroom psychology that, the next day, about ten guys adopted the look. Unfortunately, they never noticed one important detail. Herb's suspenders attached to his pants with fashionable leather straps, while most of our impressionable staff purchased the clip-on variety.

Dudnick, we soon learned, would be a strange combination of screamer, tyrant, and mensch. He was tough on me, and I deserved it. Until Herb arrived, I thought of television news departments as existing to serve my needs, not the other way around.

## Claire the Goldfish

Dudnick brought to KRON a hard-news philosophy of owning big stories. So, when San Francisco's sewer system developed a pollution problem on a Monday, we followed it the entire week. By Wednesday, the crisis had passed, but we continued covering all pertinent and potentially related dangers, real or imaginary. Again, I found myself inside the sewage plant laboratory, asking questions, piecing together yet another report about how San Franciscans could finally flush without fear.

On one of the lab's countertops, there sat a big, beautiful goldfish swimming in a bowl. "What's with the fish?" I asked.

"That's Claire," said lab boss Chuck Polling. "She's our mascot." Then he told her story.

Months earlier, a callous San Franciscan had, Polling assumed, dumped his goldfish down a toilet. Why? Who knows? Maybe he was moving. Maybe he simply didn't care. Doesn't matter. With a loud whoosh, Claire entered the bowels of the city sewer system.

Who knows how long she struggled? Who knows where Claire traveled or what horrors she witnessed? Who knows whether she was even a she? But, in San Francisco, all sewage pipes lead to the central purification plant where, before being pumped into the Pacific Ocean, material undergoes processing. Inevitably, this meant certain doom for Claire. Those machines wouldn't discern the difference between a fish and a typical piece of sewage.

Polling explained how the churning and sifting and bubbling lasts eight hours. "It happens in stages," he said. Like a giant garbage disposal, the sewage plant reduces even moderate chunks of matter into tiny particles.

Poor Claire. Toward the end of her tribulations, she entered a maze of tightly wound, high-pressure piping and fast-spinning blades known as the sludge room. The gauntlet stripped away her fins and scraped off most of her scales, but there must be a goldfish god because, miraculously, Claire remained more or less intact. She passed to the system's final stage, which plopped her, along with tons of other treated sludge, into a large outdoor settling vat called the clarifying tank.

"That's where we found her," said Polling. "And that's why we named her—Claire."

The next day, Friday, offered little in the way of breaking sewer news. I pitched Claire as a kicker to our animal-loving news director. Dudnick bought the idea and, thanks to a fortunate goldfish, I found a way out of his doghouse, at least for a while.

## CLAIRE THE GOLDFISH
### Spring 1987

[TRACK]
THIS STORY BEGINS, WHERE MOST OTHERS END . . .

[SOT]
(sound of a flushing toilet)

[TRACK]
AS CHUCK POLLING OF SAN FRANCISCO'S CLEAN
WATER DEPARTMENT TELLS US, IT'S A TALE OF
TRIUMPH, STRUGGLE, COURAGE, AND
PERSEVERANCE . . .
THE STORY OF CLAIRE, A GOLDFISH.

[SOT]
Polling: "Her fins were torn. She was missing about a
quarter of her scales. She was missing some meat and
she must have had some kind of swim bladder
damage because she was floating crooked in the
water, like that . . ." (he holds his hand upside down)

[TRACK]
CLAIRE, HE SAYS, IS THE ONLY FISH KNOWN TO
HAVE SURVIVED A TRIP THROUGH THE SAN
FRANCISCO SEWER SYSTEM.

[SOT]
(shots of sewage underground)

[TRACK]
SHE PASSED THROUGH MILES OF UNDERGROUND
TUNNELS AND WATERFALLS—
THROUGH HIGH-PRESSURE PUMPING STATIONS—
AND THEN, THIS MENACING LIFTING DEVICE CALLED
ARCHIMEDES SCREW . . .

[SOT]
(more rushing water; we look at the screw)

[TRACK]
IN ALL, CLAIRE WOULD ENDURE EIGHT HOURS OF

SEWAGE PROCESSING, INCLUDING THE SLUDGE
ROOM.

[SOT]
(natural sound in sludge room)

[SOT]
Polling: "Well you have all these pumps in here and
everything gets pushed by little propellers."

Wayne: "CLAIRE MADE IT THROUGH SLUDGE
CONTROL?"

Polling: "She was very lucky. Somehow, she passed
between all the blades of all the propellers."

[TRACK]
. . . ONLY TO FIND HERSELF EJECTED INTO THESE
HUGE SEPARATION VATS WHERE WATER GOES ONE
WAY, AND GUNK THE OTHER. THIS IS WHERE WORK
CREWS FINALLY RESCUED HER—IN THE CLARIFYING
TANK.

[SOT]
Polling: "That's why we named her."

Wayne: "CLAIRE?"

Polling: "Claire-eee-fyer, is the fish's full name."

[SOT]
We see Claire in her bowl. A finger taps on the tank.
We hear him say: "Claire . . ."

[TRACK]
AND THAT'S THE SOGGY SAGA OF A TOUGH LITTLE
FISH WHO BEAT THE ODDS AND BECAME A SEWER
SYSTEM LEGEND. NOW . . . ONE MORE QUESTION.

[SOT]
Wayne: WHAT IF SOMEBODY SEES THIS AND SAYS,
"THAT'S MY GOLDFISH; I WANT CLAIRE BACK"?

Polling: "He'll have to prove it."

# 3

## Questions and Answers: Interviewing for Sound Bites

There is one final and most important prerequisite for developing characters in television news stories. Once you find a person and convince him to talk, he must do so openly and compellingly.

In theory, reporters shouldn't care how their subjects come across, but don't believe it. The people in our stories speak to the viewers through us. It's our job to present them as faithfully as possible.

The perfect interview subject is glib, funny, or deadly serious. He's insightful, honest, energetic, articulate, and conveys his thoughts in seven-second increments. But, when we're fortunate enough to interview someone who does speak in sound bites, we immediately become suspicious. It's like agreeing to teach poker to a self-proclaimed newbie who, gosh, knows nothing about playing cards, and later walks away with the pot.

Darn us reporters. We want it all. The ideal subject is savvy, but not too savvy. He's polished, but not too smooth. He's aware of the camera but doesn't play to it. In a word, he's a natural. If you encounter such a person twice in a year you're two ahead of the next guy.

As for the rest of the people you interview, don't get your hopes up. Every day brings a television news equivalent of the amateur hour.

## Two Kinds of Sound Bites

When we strip away external factors, there are only two kinds of sound bites:

1. Sound bites presenting facts
2. Sound bites with emotional content

In the most basic of factual interviews, you might speak with a police detective who only grudgingly provides the information you need. Such conversations can quickly become a version of Twenty Questions.

You ask. He replies. You catch a clue and probe again. From negative answers, you may glean useful information. There is gamesmanship in such encounters and most reporters enjoy it, even if the verbal jockeying never makes air. That's just as well. To viewers, it would sound ridiculous:

"Is this a murder investigation?" you might ask.

"We can't comment on that at this time."

"Are homicide detectives involved?"

"We can't comment on that, either."

"If they weren't involved, could you confirm that?"

"Yes, we could confirm that, under certain circumstances."

"Is this one of those circumstances?"

"No."

"So how many homicide detectives are working the case?"

"Three."

Beyond the sporting aspects, however, reporters usually want more than facts from interviews. Facts, you see, are *our* currency. Good reporters can present them more clearly and concisely than a newsmaker.

There will be exceptions, and you'll recognize them when you hear them. Here's the test: *if a sound bite can explain a fact more efficiently, more clearly, with more drama, or with more authority than you, then, by all means, use it.*

As an example, here are the words of Franklin Delano Roosevelt on December 8, 1941, after the Japanese attacked Pearl Harbor:

> Yesterday, the Japanese also launched an attack against Malaya. Last night, Japanese forces attacked Hong Kong. Last night, Japanese forces attacked Guam. Last night, Japanese forces attacked the Philippine Islands. Last night, Japan attacked Wake Island. This morning, Japan attacked Midway Island.

That's strong stuff. Roosevelt simply stated facts, but they were powerful. We would use such a sound bite in any broadcast, then or now.

But realistically, such large moments don't happen every day. In routine news stories, factual statements can't possibly have the same impact. Those are the times when reporters look for sound bites expressing opinions, emotions, and reactions.

Here's a helpful general rule: *use facts to present a story objectively, and use interviews or sound bites to shade them subjectively.*

## The Essential Question: Why?

I heard one of the best examples of a subjective sound bite from Professor Max Utsler when he taught journalism at the University of Missouri. He told the story of a Missouri state trooper who gave interviews at the scene of a fatal hit-and-run accident. To most of the reporters, the officer spoke like a typical cop. But one woman pursued a subjective line of questioning: "You look upset. Can you step outside your uniform for a moment and tell us what bothers you most about this accident?"

"In fifteen years on the job, this is the worst I've ever seen."

"Why?" she pushed.

"The little boy's shoe," said the cop. "I found it across the high-way. That speeding car knocked him right out of his shoe. I'll see it for the rest of my life."

It was an emotional sound bite, one that amplified the facts. How, you might wonder, did that reporter break through the offi-cer's thick skin and get him to talk from the heart? Simple. Her question addressed his humanity.

Having done so, she pushed it further and asked, "Why?" Isn't that the essential question? "Why" usually reveals the most about a person or a situation. If you get to "why," your viewer will already have good sense of the who, what, when, where, and how.

Sometimes, though, it can be difficult to get any sound bites at all from the people you interview.

# Overcoming On-Camera Discomfort:
# The Elephant Trainer

As soon as Patrick Harned introduced himself, I knew we had a problem.

He mumbled.

He gave short, vague answers.

He barely looked at us. Instead, he lavished attention on an elephant named Shirley.

Patrick and his elephants had come to town as part of the circus. Its press relations people offered to let me ride one of the creatures in a parade, but news professionals have a disparaging description for reporters who participate in stories. We call it "riding the elephant." I was not about to do so literally.

We settled, instead, on a story about the elephant trainer. That's how, three hours before an evening performance, my photographer and I stood in the arena parking lot, watching Patrick wash Shirley and her elephant friends.

"Don't you get tired of being around elephants all day?"

"No, not at all," said Patrick. "Elephants don't talk back. I'm a solitary person and don't much like talking to people."

Suffice it to say, Patrick didn't come from central casting. We had gone to the circus expecting an upbeat story about a performer and, instead, got stuck with an introvert. Patrick Harned clammed up every time the camera came near. "I just like elephants," he kept saying.

"Can you explain it?" I must have asked a dozen times.

"I just do. They're unique animals, and this is a unique job. How long is this story going to be? One minute? Two?"

At that rate, it might not become a story at all, but we kept after him. We spent the afternoon following Patrick around the circus, feeling like interlopers while he said more to the elephants than to us. Had we done something to offend him? In a last effort, I addressed his reticence: "Patrick, is it that you aren't comfortable with this? If so—"

He cut me off. "Not comfortable? I'm petrified."

"Of us?"

"Well, yes." And, with this admission, Patrick Harned opened up: "I'm not very good with cameras or crowds. I know that. The elephants are great but the performing part—that's hard to come by."

Patrick confessed to having a serious case of stage fright, one that extended to us. Now his weird behavior made sense, and the explanation changed our approach. Instead of doing a piece about pampered elephants, we focused on how Patrick dealt with his awkwardness in front of a crowd.

Now that we understood one another, Patrick Harned shattered our preconceptions. Unlike other entertainers, applause meant little to him. He had taken the job to be with elephants. Show business only got in the way. "My bosses tell me I need to style better when performing," he said.

"What do you mean?"

"I don't know. That's why I have a hard time doing it."

By the time our story about the shy, reluctant performer aired, it didn't run one minute or two, but three, and reminded me of a valuable lesson. *When interviewing people, let them speak their minds.* Help them find their comfort zones.

## The Other Side of the Microphone

You're not likely to appreciate the art of interviewing until you experience it from the other side, with a microphone in your face. I've been interviewed several times. When the reporter asked perceptive questions and made me feel like the most important person in his world, I fared well. But when he cut me off, or tried to make my answers fit his expectations, I came across badly.

Lesson learned. Let an interviewee be himself.

## Disguise the Method

In Richard Ford's thoughtful novel *The Sportswriter,* his main character, Frank Bascombe, gives advice to a young intern who can't quite get the knack of interviewing. "I have a hard time asking questions," she tells him. "Mine are too complicated and no one says too much."

"You have to keep questions simple and remember to ask the same ones over and over again, sometimes in different words," replies Bascombe. "You just need to get out of their way." Even if that advice does come from a fictional character, it's absolutely true.

Accomplished interviewers make the process look easy, but that belies their efforts. They keep their questions simple and, when possible, subjective or experiential. They listen, letting their questions follow from responses. When the person does begin talking, those interviewers instinctively back off, letting the answers flow.

Most important, effective interviewers hide the method. They know that ordinary people are not born performers. Like Patrick Harned, they do best when they feel relaxed and natural. As a reporter, it's your job to help them find that frame of mind. In the same way that your subject welcomes you into his home or office, make him comfortable with shooting the story. Interviews begin long before you ask that first question.

Imagine it from your subject's perspective. Maybe you called on short notice. He's cancelled appointments and changed plans—and maybe even his clothes. You haven't asked a question and, already, you've added stress to his day.

It worsens when you arrive late. Your subject sees a brightly painted truck in his driveway, and notices the neighbors walking out to look. He hadn't anticipated creating such a commotion.

But, as the reporter, you're oblivious to his mounting concerns. Instead, you're angry with the photographer for not driving faster, while he's miffed about having missed lunch. Your subject reads the tension.

Then, as the interview begins, your photographer turns on a bright bulb mounted atop his rig, unintentionally blinding your subject. It's the crucial moment and he freezes, becoming a human version of that deer caught in the headlights. Can you blame him?

## Microphones

How then, can you make interviews less obtrusive? Begin with your microphone selection.

Try to avoid the handheld variety, particularly if your station has adorned them with fancy logos. Sticks, as we call them, work best when you're in a hurry or shooting in environments with loud background noise—places like busy streets. Handheld microphones clutter your photographer's artful pictures. They get in the way of intelligent conversations. How can a person feel relaxed when you continually point a microphone and take it away? The reporter has the power and the subject knows it.

Instead, try to use a wireless lapel microphone. From a production perspective, wireless microphones are excellent for capturing natural sound. They move with your subject, hearing almost everything.

Go so far as to help your subject attach it. In this simple but tactile way, both of you work together on a small project before the interview even begins. By entering his personal space, you subliminally demonstrate that you don't bite. It sounds corny, but it works.

Additionally, as long as he wears that microphone, the interview continues, albeit in a more casual manner. Every question becomes progressively less threatening, allowing your subject more time to open up.

## Thirty-five Feet of Honesty

Ray Farkas, formerly of NBC News and now a freelance producer, has turned interviewing into a science, often with visually stunning results. Years ago, Farkas grew weary of traditional question-and-answer techniques. "As soon as you turn on the camera, a subject figuratively clears his throat and the voice drops an octave," Farkas says. "The whole idea is to reduce intimidation. Make a person unaware that these could be his fifteen minutes—or, more likely, his fifteen seconds—of fame."

To that end, Farkas might place the camera twenty, thirty, or forty feet away, shooting through doors and windows, across streets, and around plants. At forty feet, instead of the more conventional five feet, Farkas gets what he calls "Thirty-five more feet of honesty. When they can't see the camera, they're less influenced or intimidated by it."

## Lights, or No Lights?

For the same reason, Farkas avoids using lights when possible. "One light begets two, then three, and with each additional one, the environment becomes more artificial," he says. "With the quality of cameras these days, we can get pictures from almost anywhere. What you gain in image quality from the lights, you lose in humanity. I want to get as close to that humanity as possible. Boost the gain switch on the camera, instead."

## Positioning

Even when Farkas reverts to a more standard interview, he pays particular attention to body language and positioning. You'll rarely see his subjects facing directly toward the camera. If they're sitting, Farkas turns their chairs by as much as ninety degrees in relation to the camera lens. "It changes the look. If a guy's sitting straight on, it makes a boring shot. But when you rotate the chair, a person must lean in toward the camera. It's the same as being in a bar. People don't face each other on barstools. One person turns his head to the other."

Farkas adds a note of caution, though, about placing an interview subject in a location as if he were a prop. "It might make a nice shot, but if a person looks or feels awkward, it defeats the purpose. The interview reflects that."

As a general rule, compromise the shot before you compromise a subject's psychological or personal comfort. Reporters and photographers will always have battles of wills about this, and should try to find a mutual medium.

## Eye Contact

People make eye contact almost every time they speak, but it's doubly important when interviewing. Try to put yourself at eye level, just to the right or the left of the lens plane, and move as close to the person as possible without intruding into the frame. Look directly into your subject's eyes for both questions and answers. When you connect at that level, you engage the entire person. People are less likely to worry about a camera if they don't look at it.

## Keep Your Sound Bites Fresh

It's only natural that people to be interviewed want to know, "What are we going to talk about? What will you ask me?" Reporters hear those questions almost every day.

Don't be too specific in your reply. "Nothing we didn't talk about on the telephone," I usually tell them, and leave it at that. Here's why. *People tend to give their best answers and descriptions when they know a listener hasn't heard them before.* It's human nature. Besides, no reporter wants to edit around phrases like "As I said earlier . . ." Keep that in mind, and be careful not to lose your sound bites before the camera rolls.

The late Charles Kuralt of CBS News described this as *keeping a sound bite fresh.*

Don't misunderstand. I'm not suggesting you ignore someone before an interview. Quite the contrary: Establish a rapport. Try to get him talking about himself. Ask what he's done, what he enjoys, where he's been, or what he believes. With any of those four topics, you should be able to get someone talking within thirty seconds.

# Extracting Answers

Once your subjects are relaxed and comfortable, you still need to extract good, usable sound bites. Because you're looking for ten-second segments rather than whole conversations, though, the answers matter more than the questions. This opens up a whole range of possibilities.

## Adapt to Your Subject—Time Your Questions

As you prepare for an interview, listen carefully to how a subject speaks. Notice the patterns. You don't want to interrupt an answer. Nor do you want to lose a potentially good sound bite by letting a statement hang. If an answer sounds incomplete, a well-timed verbal nudge might help your subject finish it.

Read the person. Notice whether he's low-key or high-strung. Adjust accordingly. Anticipate the conversational tone to which your subject will best respond. Some people need sympathy. Others like to be teased. Be anything but bland.

When the San Francisco Giants went to the World Series in 2002, we did a piece about fair-weather fans buying memorabilia. "The Benito Santiago jerseys are already sold out," moaned a woman who was shopping for her son. Santiago, the Giants' catcher, had just won most valuable player honors in the league championships. "I absolutely must have an item with 'Santiago' written on it. Anything will do." She paused. We were about to lose the conversational momentum.

"Would you settle for a map of Chile?" I quipped.

"I thought Benito Santiago was from Puerto Rico."

Because I asked a ridiculous question, she gave a sound bite that fit the mood and the moment.

## Challenge Your Subjects

Don't be afraid to challenge people, no matter what the circumstances. If a subject sounds flat, boring, or too rehearsed, play devil's advocate. With a well-placed needle at the proper time, you can become an enabler as much as an interviewer.

Try a good-natured "Aw, c'mon" sometime. Use the question as you would a can opener. Give it a twist, and your subject may pour himself out.

If necessary, you can always apologize later.

Ray Farkas remembers an interview that he conducted while producing a segment about a multiple murderer. The district attorney avoided straight answers by speaking in legalese. Eventually, Farkas tried another approach. "You must have seen worse people. Deep down, is this suspect really such a bad person? C'mon."

The DA took that question as a personal challenge. He erupted, laying into the defendant. Farkas got his sound bite.

## Ask Pointed Questions

Give a person an excuse to talk, and often he will. In 2002, a San Francisco area woman accused a professional football player and two of his friends of gang-raping her during a date. She admitted having sex with them, but only, she said, because they drugged her. After the first day's court testimony, which included stories of all-night clubs, limousines, and parties, it became clear that neither the football player and his friends nor the young woman would ever qualify as Sunday-school role models.

Defense attorney William Dubois played it safe when our interview began. "My client believed the woman was being cooperative," he said.

After such a colorless answer, I pressed him for something better. "Let's be honest. Your client admits to being a player with the ladies. That won't exactly make him sympathetic to a jury. So what can you do to turn his image around?"

Mr. Dubois made no attempt at moral apologies. "This is not a gathering of saints," he said. "Not the plaintiff, and not the defendants. These are all people whose idea of fun is to go out to clubs, get loaded, get laid, and go to work the next day. My client is just one of the many intoxicated people who wind up in bed together at the end of the evening."

Some sound bites are too darn good for a general audience.

## Interviewing Politicians

Some of your more challenging interviews will be with politicians. They're even more elusive than lawyers.

The toughest of politicians remind me of the bad police robot in *Terminator II.* Remember that scene in which it chases Arnold Schwarzenegger down the hall? Arnold shoots the robot. It falls down, staggers to its feet, the bullet hole heals itself, and the bad robot resumes its dogged pursuit. Many politicians act much the same way during interviews.

They aren't really robots, of course, but they do, at times, speak as if they've been programmed. Watch the national political shows and analyze how a politician applies spin control. You may get the impression he cares more about looking and sounding good than answering tough questions.

I have the cynical view that most politicians like reporters only when we enhance their image. They view us as a means of staying in the public eye. In interviews, politicians have agendas, just as reporters do. They already know what they want to say, and the areas they want to avoid. When politicians don't like questions, they're adept at tailoring rambling, unusable answers. In the same way politicians make themselves quotable, they also know how to make themselves *un*quotable.

You'll have an excellent chance of getting good sound bites from politicians when you know your facts, shoot straight, and, as with that bad police robot, knock them a little off-balance. When they apply spin control, politely remind them that they never answered the question, and ask again. The next time, they'll be less likely to mess with you.

There may be other times when politicians know too much for their own good. Once, Congresswoman Nancy Pelosi spent more than a minute detailing a fine point of foreign policy. She was passionate. She was persuasive. She was not trying to be evasive, but, while her answer would have been good for a live Sunday-morning network broadcast, it would never fit into our short piece.

Clearly, Pelosi wanted to make her point, and we wanted to hear it. But, as I asked the question two or three ways and then tried not to interrupt, both of us became frustrated. I had a job to do, and so did she. Finally, I took a deep breath and said, "This is a very important point. I wish we could run all of it. But at the risk of sounding shallow, how do we boil this into ten or twelve seconds?"

It was unorthodox, but it worked, and Pelosi delivered.

## Be Tactful: Jim Stolpa

There will be times, however, when you serve the story better by taking an indirect approach. You might remember Jim and Jennifer Stolpa and their infant son, Clayton. They're the family that, during a blizzard in 1992, tried to find a shortcut through California's Sierra Nevada. On a narrow mountain road, miles from any home or hamlet, they got lost, and then stuck.

As the storm worsened, the couple grew weary of waiting, swaddled the baby in a sleeping bag, and set out on foot. But, after a day, Jennifer couldn't go farther. Jim used his Army survival training to build her a cave in the snow, and then pressed ahead, alone. After nine days, he stumbled down to civilization, leading rescuers back to his wife and son.

But their ordeal wasn't over. When they arrived at the hospital in Reno, Nevada, the Stolpas found a media mob waiting. The search had made them front-page news, household names, and heroes. Although Jim and Jennifer both lost toes to frostbite, young Clayton survived unharmed. At the peak of their fame, Jim and Jennifer Stolpa became a movie of the week.

Then they disappeared from public life.

Nine years later, we became curious and traced the couple to Milwaukee, Wisconsin, for a follow-up. They had divorced, but remained good friends.

Going in, I had one difficult question to ask. During the search, it had been only natural for some people to take the name Stolpa and precede or replace it with the word "stupid." Had Jim and Jennifer ever heard about that? Could I pose the question tactfully?

I hoped Jim would address it himself, and waited for an opportunity during the interview. As we recollected media coverage, I asked, "What do you imagine the world thought about you and Jennifer at that time? What do you think people said?"

"Oh, we were stupid," he answered. "What we did was stupid, stupid, stupid. And it was. We've admitted it. But, after making a bad decision, we did everything right."

Jim gestured to Clayton, then nine years old. "I made it because of him," he said. "Clayton is the reason we survived. He's the proof. And his little sister? She's the celebration of it."

That sound bite came from asking an honest question, not a tough one. Jim had heard the talk, and wanted to address it. Jim Stolpa was hardly stupid.

## Interviewing Victims: The Salcido Murders

Reporters face their most difficult moments when asked to interview friends or families of victims. In the most trying of these assignments, we must put aside our sense of what feels proper, and knock on a door.

In 1988, a Napa, California, winery worker named Ramone Salcido killed his wife during a jealous, cocaine-induced rage. But it didn't stop there. He also cut the throats of his three young daughters, killing two of them. Next, he drove several miles to the town of Cotati and did more of the same to his in-laws and their children.

Northern California hadn't seen a crime this brutal in a long time. At KRON-TV, we went to nonstop coverage. I spent the afternoon outside the in-laws' house, around which police stretched their yellow tape. The neighbors clustered, energized by the excitement. Only later, when the coroner carried bloody body bags through the glare of television lights, did those neighbors realize the graphic mayhem that had taken place inside.

The next morning, photographer John Laursen and I returned to the neighborhood for reactions. We didn't go by choice; follow-up stories about crimes and victims feel tawdry and exploitative.

We parked on the street at noon and, unlike the day before, found a neighborhood devoid of people. Toys sat abandoned on porches, morning papers remained in driveways, and tricycles sat on the curbs. It might as well have been the rapture.

On all of Lakeview Avenue, we heard only one sound—someone practicing piano inside a house two doors down from the murders. We knocked. A woman came to the screen, but didn't open it.

"We're with NewsCenter 4." I said. "We know this is a terrible time, but we were hoping someone might tell us about the family and children down the street—what were they like?"

The woman resisted. Who wouldn't? But after a few minutes she agreed to talk, and stepped outside. As we pinned the microphone I realized what a telling shot John would get if she went back in, letting the door close. The woman did. That image of her face, diffused by the screen, said more than words ever could about sadness and vulnerability. "How could this happen to little angels?" asked the woman. "If those girls could have grown wings, they would have."

As happens so often in difficult circumstances, that first interview drew other people who also wanted to speak. Not once did we ask, "How do you feel?" Certainly, we'd come to answer that question, but those specific words, "How do you feel?" haven't any class or dignity. They make us look bad. Find a different way to phrase them.

"What do you remember about the family?"

"How long had they lived here?"

"What did they wear to trick-or-treat last Halloween?"

With some people, we didn't need to ask anything. The mood was such that, after setting a shot, it took only a look or a nod to start them talking.

## The Girl with the Red Ball

After half an hour, we had more material than we could use, but then a young girl walked up. She clutched a big red ball to her chest and, like the rest, asked to speak. Her mother approved, so why not? "What will you remember best about them?" I began.

"It wouldn't be a regular day if you didn't see them walking their little dog, Chiquita, up and down the street and smiling at everybody they saw," replied the little girl, who seemed wise and soulful beyond her years. Her words hung there, along with the image they described. In the uncomfortable pause before I could ask another question, she kept talking. "Every movie that I see, people die in them, but I never thought about how, in real life, they really die, die. Then they're just gone. You can't replace them."

By accident, the best question had been no question at all.

# Interviewing Children: Art Linkletter

The girl with the ball might have been ten years old. It's worth noting her age, because ten-year-olds make excellent if not the best interviews. They're just on the cusp of sophistication, old enough to articulate their ideas, but still young enough to be cute, innocent, honest, and respectful of their elders. At ten they haven't copped an attitude yet. Keep this in mind the next time you do a segment with elementary school kids. Ask for the fifth graders.

I base the theory on both professional and personal experiences. During the 1960s, long before syndicated programs filled our afternoon airwaves with titillating distractions, CBS ran a noontime program called *Art Linkletter's House Party.* He always spent his last few minutes by interviewing schoolkids. Linkletter was a master at it.

In 1965, *Art Linkletter's House Party* called my school and my fifth-grade teacher, Mrs. Sherock, selected me to be interviewed. On the big day, we rode to CBS Television City in a black Cadillac limousine with fins. Mr. Linkletter met us for brief pre-interviews and, about an hour later, put us in front of a studio audience. In a situation where we might have felt uncomfortable, he made it easy.

At the writing of this book, Linkletter was eighty-nine years old. Except for Santa Claus, no one in the world can claim to know more about interviewing children—he's interviewed twenty-six thousand of them. Because I had something of an "in" with the man, I telephoned him to see what he thought of my theory about ten-year-olds.

"It depends on what you want." According to Linkletter, types of answers vary with age. He compared maturity levels to foods from a buffet. "At ten, they know more. They don't have attitudes, yet. But I think younger children are more interesting because of their limited knowledge. If they don't know an answer, they may strike out wildly and say anything."

"If you had to pick one age group, what would it be?" I asked.

"Five-year-olds, because they think so directly."

Linkletter recalled asking a kindergartner if she knew her birthday. "July 15," the little girl said.

"What year?"

"Every year," she replied with conviction.

Clearly, Linkletter loved the younger kids; he kept on and on about them. He recalled asking a four-year-old boy, "Do you go to Sunday school?"

"Yes," the kid replied.

"What religion are you?"

"We're either Catholic or Prostitute."

That answer, said Linkletter, drew a big laugh from the audience, but he didn't dare join in. "No matter what a child says, keep a straight face. Be a friend. Never let him feel as if you're making fun. You'll lose him if you do."

He gave another example, of a nine-year-old boy. "What would you do if you were flying an airplane and all four engines stopped?" Linkletter asked.

"I would tell the passengers to fasten their seat belts. Then I would parachute and jump out." The audience roared, but Linkletter says he kept a straight face. It paid off because then the kid tried to reassure him. "Don't worry," he said. "I'd just be going for gas."

## Meet the Child at His Level

When interviewing a child of any age, try to meet him at his level. Be wary of intimidating him with your height; you don't want to come across as an authority figure. I remember how Linkletter's show placed kids on elevated stools. He worked us close, leaning in to make absolute eye contact, much the same as I do with people today. Maybe the example came from him.

When you meet a child, be friendly, calm, and reassuring. Use a quiet voice and ask if it's all right to talk. Empower him. Expect the child to be nervous, so begin with easy questions. Ask his name and age. Once he hears his own voice, he'll gain confidence and loosen up.

Most important, keep the interview light and upbeat. A few years ago, while doing a Thanksgiving story with some preschool students, I played dumb: "Where do turkeys come from?"

"Eggs," said one little girl.

"What kind of eggs?"

"Chickens."

"What do you do with the turkey after you've eaten it?"

"My daddy puts the turkey bones on his head," she said.

"Why would he do that?"

"He wears it like a hat!"

## Choosing the Child

Having settled on an age group, you must decide which children to interview. Linkletter applied a simple but effective method. "We didn't want the model students," he said. "We wanted the trouble-makers. We liked the kids with spunk."

To that end, Linkletter's staff always mailed the same letter to schools. "It asked the dear teachers to give us the four children they would most like to have out of the class for a few blessed hours. The teachers would laugh and send me the rascals."

Imagine my disappointment. I always figured Mrs. Sherock sent me to Art Linkletter as some kind of reward. And now we know that it had been, but not for me—for her.

# Interviewing Older People and Veterans: The B-17

Mr. Linkletter finished our talk by describing the time he asked an octogenarian to give him one good reason for living to be a hundred. "There's no peer pressure," the woman replied.

If only our elders were always so easy to interview. You may have heard the remarkable tale of Charles Brown, who piloted a B-17 during World War II. In 1943, while flying his first mission over Bremen, Germany, enemy fire knocked Brown's bomber into a five-mile death spiral. Brown blacked out during the plunge, but, with seconds to spare, he awoke and pulled the plane to straight and level flight. "I still have recurring nightmares about seeing those trees out my windshield," he says.

But Brown's crisis was only beginning. Of the plane's four engines, just one remained running. He'd lost most of the plane's tail to cannon fire, along with the plastic bombardier's bubble. Consequently, a fierce winter wind blew through the fuselage, freezing the surviving crewmembers and their guns.

Having righted the plane, Brown still believed he could get it home, but then he flew directly over a Luftwaffe fighter base. "My heart sank."

Minutes later, an ME-109 fighter intercepted to make the kill. Its pilot, Franz Steigler, had already shot down two B-17s that day. A third would give him the Knight's Cross. But, as Steigler closed, he saw blood on the windows. He saw the motionless guns. He saw how the plane teetered to stay aloft. He moved closer and locked eyes with Charles Brown.

"What did you see in them?" I asked Steigler.

"Fear."

It was December 22, three days before Christmas, and, in that moment, Franz Steigler made a personal decision. He knew the war would end someday, and how he would have to look himself in the mirror if he survived. "I thought of myself as a warrior, not a murderer."

Instead of shooting, Steigler tried to force Brown into landing. When he refused, the German escorted him halfway home across the North Sea, saluting as they parted. "If he could make it back in that plane in that condition, he deserved to live," said Steigler.

Later, Brown made a miracle landing at Kimbolton, England. His superiors promised the Congressional Medal of Honor, but, when Brown continued praising the German pilot who spared his life, they changed their minds and buried his report inside top-secret files, where it remained for forty years. Back in Germany, Steigler also kept the story to himself, for fear of being court-martialed. But he always wondered about that B-17.

And so did Charles Brown. He survived twenty-six more missions, made a career in the Air Force, and spent almost five decades searching for the man who spared him.

In 1990, when they finally found each other, I covered their reunion for CBS News. The men spent two days at an Army Air Corps get-together near Boston. They visited a B-17, shared beers, and discovered a kinship beyond the original incident. It often works out this way. Former enemies find they have more in common with each other than with anyone outside their circle.

But they didn't open up to us. Perhaps it comes from a mindset born of sacrifices, but many World War II veterans tend to be difficult interviews. They have plenty to say, but seem reluctant to say it. When talking about the war, most hide their feelings. Whenever one of them comes close to sharing his emotions, it seems as if he pulls back and says something like, "Well, it was just tough. We did what we had to do."

This is a frustrating trait. Steigler, Brown, and the rest of Brown's crew talked, but they didn't give us the emotional kind of sound bites that you read above, or that we needed. Steigler remained stoic. Brown took refuge in facts. Somehow, I had to crack them out of the present and capture the intensity of their encounter so many years earlier.

We began with Charles. Instead of opening with the crucial questions, I pressed him for details, hoping to make memories of that day more vivid.

"What was the weather like?"

"Do you remember what you had for breakfast?"

"Who was your copilot?"

"Did you bring along a good luck charm?"

Our conversation assumed a pattern of questions and answers.

"How long were you above the ball bearing factory in Bremen?"

"What does a guy worry about on his first mission?"

"What does flak sound like?"

We continued—question, answer, question, answer, question, answer—and then, as he described the moment when his B-17 began to fall, I let the statement hang and didn't ask anything. Charles expected another question. When he didn't hear it, he assumed he should keep talking. In the way a roller coaster peaks and then enters free-fall, Charles Brown finally told his story with unguarded passion. His voice cracked. Tears welled in his eyes. "We flew for different sides," he said, "But still, the code, the honor was there."

As difficult as Brown had been, Steigler proved tougher still. After a similar thread of questions, the elderly German never came close to cracking.

Ultimately, we broke through with visual and tactile cues. Before shooting the story I'd asked Brown, along with his surviving crewmembers, to bring along names and photographs of their children, grandchildren, and great-grandchildren.

Toward the end of our interview with Steigler, I recalled the names and photos and, as a last resort, handed them to the stoic old pilot. "Do you know who they are?"

He did.

"Could you look at the pictures and read the names, please." Franz Steigler complied. He had never seen them before. When he took the pictures and read the roll call of men, women, boys, and girls, he finally realized the consequences of his act. Those people had come into being and lived that day because, on a fearful afternoon three days before Christmas almost half a century earlier, he didn't pull the trigger.

The old pilot held the photographs, looking stunned. "Well, it's fate," he stammered while shaking his head. "And fate is something we have no control about."

Don't believe a word of it. Charles Brown never will.

# 4

## Narrative Structure: Beginnings, Middles, Endings, and Timelines

Young reporters ask me one question time and again. "How do I write more creatively?"

Here's the answer. Manipulate a story's timeline to give it a distinct beginning, middle and ending. That's simplistic, so please bear with the explanation. This is technical, but fundamental.

What is a timeline? Every story has three of them:

1. The order of events as they unfold
2. The order in which you record them
3. The order in which you present those events to the viewer

The third of those timelines is the most important. It's also where your fun and creativity begin.

Let's look at a hypothetical example: the story of Bill Johnson, an emergency dispatcher who, by giving Heimlich instructions over the telephone, saved a victim's life. Assume you arrive at the dispatch center to shoot a piece for the late news and have these limited elements with which to work:

1. Johnson at his console
2. An interview with him
3. A recording of the emergency telephone conversation
4. Pictures of the hospital

You do not have pictures or interviews with the victim, nor with the person whom the dispatcher helped on the phone. How would you structure the story?

Here's your first option, a straightforward linear timeline in which the story begins before the emergency call:

> [TRACK]
> IN HIS TEN YEARS AS AN EMERGENCY DISPATCHER,
> BILL JOHNSON NEVER HAD A NIGHT LIKE THIS.
>
> [SOT]
> Emergency tape: "Help! Help! My friend is choking!"
>
> [TRACK]
> THE CALL CAME FROM A CAR PHONE . . .

Now, a second option. In this one, we begin the story later, with recorded sound of the emergency call:

> [SOT]
> Emergency tape: "Help! Help! My friend is choking!"
>
> [TRACK]
> THE CALL CAME FROM A CAR PHONE . . .

[SOT]
Bill Johnson: "The guy had maybe a minute to
live."

[TRACK]
HE'D BEEN EATING CHICKEN WINGS WHILE RIDING
IN A CAR . . .

Finally, as a third option, consider beginning the story at the end of the event timeline, with its outcome. Because you arrived late and have limited elements, this allows you to open with the newest information:

[TRACK]
WHEN BILL JOHNSON FINISHES WORK, HE OFTEN
KNOWS HE'S HELPED SAVED A LIFE . . . BUT IT
NEVER HAPPENED LIKE THIS . . .

[SOT]
Emergency tape: "Help! Help! My friend is choking!"

[SOT]
Bill Johnson: "It wasn't a typical call . . ."

[TRACK]
THE CALL CAME FROM A DRIVER ON INTERSTATE
580. HE AND A FRIEND HAD BEEN EATING CHICKEN
WINGS WHILE ON THE ROAD . . .

Each version creates an element of suspense. This last one gives viewers enough information to expect a happy ending, but keeps them wondering how it came about.

# Choosing Your Structural Timeline

So now you see how even a simple story can present multiple structural options. In deciding which to use, ask yourself the following questions:

1. *Is it hard news or a feature?* The harder the news story, the more quickly you must get to the point.
2. *Which is more compelling, the facts, or the way those facts developed—or possibly the video?* Try to open with your strongest material. In a feature, that may mean romancing the open a little to let the piece develop.
3. *How much time do you have?* You can't put as much structural nuance into a ninety-second story as you would into a longer piece. Shorter stories usually require that you write in a more direct line.
4. *Will anchors introduce the piece from the studio, or will you front it from the field in a live shot?* To accommodate your time live on camera, packages generally run a little shorter. In such circumstances, you may choose to save a couple of details for use in the live transitions.

Weigh all of these factors, then write the piece.

## The Almost-Perfect Crash

In 1984, the Federal Aviation Administration experimented with a gelatinous jet-fuel additive called Antimisting Kerosene. In theory, if a plane crashed, the Antimisting Kerosene in its tanks would prevent the fuel from spraying and exploding.

To test it, the FAA and NASA rigged an old four-engine Boeing 720 airliner for remote control flight. Scientists planned to fill the plane's tanks with the new fuel and then to crash it. They gave the exercise one of those fancy acronyms—CID, for Controlled Impact

Demonstration—and invited members of the press to Edwards Air Force Base, in California's Mojave Desert, where they would watch.

Before dawn, and with typical military efficiency, the FAA shepherded more than a hundred reporters through a maze of high-security dirt roads, and delivered us to a mountaintop overlooking the test area. Once there, we spent several hours waiting and shivering.

To help us produce our stories, NASA and the FAA handed out videotape of the preparations. It included pictures of technicians strapping doomed test dummies into airline seats before their final, fateful rides.

At long last, the remotely controlled plane took off, circled the valley, and began its final approach. On impact, it would twist and careen into a nearby steel structure designed to rip the wing tanks, spray fuel, and create sparks. Under such conditions, a plane loaded with regular fuel would easily blow up.

This plane wasn't supposed to.

But what we saw from that mountain played out like a slow-motion nightmare. As planned, the airliner descended, dipped its left wing, and slapped to the ground in a cloud of dust. Then, as the jet twisted into the wing-ripping structure, the fuel spilled out and— *kaboom!* It blew into smithereens. So much for Antimisting Kerosene. We felt the rumbling shockwaves from two miles away. The fireball made spectacular video. NASA cameras captured it from several angles, both outside and inside the plane. Those test dummies never had a chance. (You can see the crash on the Internet at *www.dfrc.nasa.gov/gallery/photo/CID.*)

When it came time to write, the material offered several structural possibilities, but it made sense that we should use as much of the spectacular crash video as possible. So, rather than using a linear timeline, I opted for a structure in which we showed different shots of the impact at the beginning, in the middle, and at the end.

The story begins late along the event timeline, only a few seconds before impact. For the first shot, we used a point-of-view angle of the plane approaching a NASA camera mounted atop the wing-ripper. Viewers see the plane wobble and dive, clearly about to auger in. The piece begins with one sentence:

> [TRACK]
> IT WAS AN ALMOST PERFECT LANDING . . .

As the jet pancakes into the ground and blows up, we let the natural sound play full. That sets the scene. Here are the other elements, in the order we used them:

1. The preparations, including dummy installations
2. The takeoff
3. Historical footage of other fatal crashes
4. Shots of the test dummies at impact
5. Reactions from the scientists
6. More crash pictures, this time from a camera mounted on the plane's tail
7. A stand-up bridge, summarizing the day's events
8. One final, well-cut crash sequence

For a last line, I made a distinction between perfect tests, and imperfect results.

# Fundamentals of Structure

In even the earliest days of language, our ancestors sat around campfires and told stories. They might have described the day's hunt—how they awoke early, crossed the river, found tracks, closed on the prey, made the kill, and returned home with dinner. If you examine the essentials of that one sentence, you'll notice how it begins, has a middle and an ending, has characters, has tension and resolution, and tells a story.

The biggest difference between those old days and now is that our campfire has evolved into television. Instead of a few people gathered around, there are tens of thousands, if not millions. But here's the tradeoff: When we tell stories, we don't see our audience. Sometimes we forget it even exists.

## Set a Scene

When you tell a story to a friend, how do you begin? If you're like most people, you probably sell it a little. You engage the listener's interest and take it from there. Try to do the same in television news. Set a scene with a line or two, or possibly three.

You might recall a mishap involving San Francisco newspaper publisher Phil Bronstein, also known as Mr. Sharon Stone. Bronstein is a reptile fan, and, in the summer of 2001, his actress wife made a large donation to the Los Angeles Zoo. In gratitude, zoo officials granted the couple a special tour inside a cage containing a ten-foot-long Komodo dragon, the most rare and ferocious of carnivorous lizards.

Before Bronstein entered that cage, zookeepers asked him to remove his shoes and socks. He did, much to the delight of the Komodo dragon, which dined on a four-by-two-inch section of Bronstein's big toe area. It dispatched the publisher not only to the hospital, but also into his own headlines.

Although the Komodo mauling took place in Los Angeles, we gave it big play in San Francisco. Thankfully, several Los Angeles stations covered the attack and shared their video. Still, from our perspective, most of those stories missed the spirit of it. I'll paraphrase one reporter's opening. He began with a tight shot of the lizard's gaping jaws and razor-sharp teeth:

[TRACK]
AT THE LOS ANGELES ZOO, OFFICIALS SAY THEY ARE
SURPRISED AND PUZZLED HOW THIS RARE
KOMODO DRAGON ATTACKED A SAN FRANCISCO
NEWSPAPER PUBLISHER LAST NIGHT . . .

There was nothing wrong with that open, but the reporter wasn't particularly creative, either. Although his writing was safe, it didn't sizzle. The reporter might as well have been describing a press conference.

Here is my opening line, using the same video:

[TRACK]
THIS IS THE MOUTH—
THAT MUNCHED ON THE BIG TOE—
THAT IS ATTACHED TO THE RIGHT FOOT—
OF THE MAN WHO IS LEGALLY ATTACHED TO
ACTRESS SHARON STONE . . .

Which sets a scene better?

Which establishes the proper mood?

## Scene Sets Are Narrative

Good storytelling means engaging the viewers. We refer to our scripts as "tracks," but by that we really mean *narration*, which derives from the word "narrative" and implies, in turn, a relationship between the storyteller and his audience.

It harks back to the campfire and the hunt. In the oral tradition, a good storyteller keeps listeners hanging on every word. But, in television news, reporters are rarely as successful. They forget to let the facts work for them.

David Busse, a photographer at KABC-TV in Los Angeles, recalls working a story about the search for a missing three-year-old child.

When investigators began to suspect she had been abducted and killed, they went to a landfill and looked for a body.

For two days, Busse and others shot distant video of the searchers. But, just before deadline on the second day, authorities allowed a pool camera to get close-up shots of the workers sifting through the landfill trash. "They weren't really gripping pictures," said Busse, "Unless the words to accompany them made them gripping."

Most of the reporters wrote leads that went something like this:

> [TRACK]
> MORE THAN A HUNDRED WORKERS CONTINUED THE
> SEARCH OF MIRAMAR LANDFILL LOOKING FOR ANY
> SIGNS OF THREE-YEAR-OLD . . .

But Busse's reporter, Jaie Avila, wrote a lead line that spoke to the mood and the moment:

> [TRACK]
> THE ONLY THING WORSE THAN THE WORK WAS THE
> THOUGHT OF WHAT THEY MIGHT FIND . . .

Both lines were factually correct. But which will stay with you?

## Lead Viewers into the Story

Here is the open to a piece about San Francisco's annual cable-car bell-ringing championships. Note the quick timeline jumps— from the morning, to two days earlier, to later that afternoon— and how the tracks invite viewers to make their own discoveries. In the first sequence, they see the defending champion as he arrives at the contest:

> [TRACK]
> WHEN BYRON COBB FINALLY SHOWED AT
> FISHERMAN'S WHARF TODAY, IT WASN'T SO MUCH
> AN ARRIVAL AS AN ENTRANCE . . .

[SOT]
Guys greet Byron. They slap hands:
"How's it going, baby?"
"Bring it on!"

[TRACK]
SUCH IS THE BURDEN OF EXPECTATIONS, AND THE
ROLE OF A CHAMPION, BECAUSE MEN WITH TITLES
ALSO BECOME TARGETS.

[SOT]
(file tape from two days earlier: a cable car passes,
ringing bell . . .)

[TRACK]
ALONG THE CALIFORNIA STREET CABLE-CAR LINE,
BYRON'S RIVALS WATCH HIM 364 DAYS A YEAR . . .
AND THEN, ON THE 365th, THEY TAKE AIM . . .

Based on that open, would you want to see who wins the contest?

## Setting the Scene in a Longer Story

In 1992, photographer Pam Partee and I traveled Route 66 and
stopped in what remained of Chambers, Arizona. There, we profiled a die-hard desert recluse named Nyal Rockwell, who owned a
wrecking business and roadhouse called Rocky's. He'd moved to
Chambers in the 1950s when "the Old Road," as they call it, still
carried traffic.

Rocky's did brisk business for more than a decade, but, when the
federal government replaced Route 66 with Interstate 40, life along
that corridor changed. As part of the new highway deal, the feds
promised to build an off-ramp into Chambers. Alas, the government never delivered—at least, not to Nyal Rockwell's satisfaction.

"How far is it from the off-ramp to here?" I asked as we walked along a chainlink fence at the back of his property.

"Five miles down and five miles back," Rockwell answered. "Ten miles round trip."

And yet, from that fence we could feel the wind from traffic rushing past on Interstate 40. Those cars were less than twenty feet away, but for Nyal Rockwell they might as well have been in another galaxy.

When, predictably, Interstate 40 turned Chambers into a ghost town, Nyal Rockwell stayed behind—angry, stubborn, and still waiting for his off-ramp. Aside from his sickly, loyal wife and a collection of rusting cars with fins, Rocky's was all he had. Nyal clung to it.

The piece opens with shots of the old abandoned highway. We show the remnants of a derelict church, and then cut to a tight shot of a rotting plywood sign out front. You can barely make out the meeting times. We used that sign, and others, as a theme. The scene set also serves as a prologue:

> [TRACK]
> ACCORDING TO THE SIGN, THERE WILL BE WORSHIP
> AT THE CHAMBERS PENTECOSTAL CHURCH THIS
> SUNDAY, BUT, FROM THE LOOK OF THINGS, ONLY
> TERMITES WILL ATTEND.
>
> (pictures of an old gas station)
>
> [TRACK]
> NOT FAR AWAY, ANOTHER SIGN SAYS THEY STILL
> SELL GAS FOR THIRTY-EIGHT CENTS A GALLON.
>
> (we dissolve again to a shot of peeling signs along
> the road)

[TRACK]
BUT, ON ROUTE 66, SIGNS MAY BE DECEIVING.
THEY HAVE A WAY OF POINTING TO THE PAST, NOT
THE FUTURE. . . .

(we see Nyal Rockwell holding a metal road sign)

[SOT]
Nyal: "Can you read that? National Old Trails Road,
it says."

(we dissolve to a compression shot of a dusty dirt
road)

[TRACK]
NEAR CHAMBERS, THE NATIONAL OLD TRAILS ROAD
IS A DIRT PATH BUMPING OUT OF THE DESERT.
IT IS THE TRAIL THAT BEGAT ROUTE 66. . . .
THAT BEGAT INTERSTATE 40 . . .
THAT BEGAT THE SAD ENDING OF NYAL ROCKWELL'S
WRECKING BUSINESS AND ROADHOUSE. . . .

For what it's worth, I could work fifty more years and never write a
better open. It delivers viewers into a place and a time, and establishes a mood.

# Using Structure to Craft a Package: Joey's Scrapbook

Here's a trade secret—with a proper beginning and ending, the
middle of a story will usually take care of itself. You'll always find it
easier to write a piece if, before leaving a location, you already know
how it will start and finish. Think of this as planning your entrance
and exit routes.

There is no better example than the story we did about a Memorial Day lunch. Jack's Grill in San Francisco wanted to honor the families of Vietnam veterans killed in action. The manager anticipated more than a hundred people, but, when photographer Doug Laughlin and I arrived, we found less than twenty.

It didn't look like much of a story.

We interviewed a few family members and started to leave, but then I spotted an elderly woman, Gloria Dougherty, holding tightly to a scrapbook. On a hunch, I asked her about it, and she began to talk. Those pages told the full life story of her son, Joey Artavia. She showed us his birth certificate, his death certificate, and most everything in between.

Mrs. Dougherty had deep, sad eyes. She clutched that book as if Joey himself might still be inside. From one short interview, she gave us three very good sound bites and came across as a strong character, but to make this a complete story it needed a beginning and ending.

"Where are you going after this?" I asked Mrs. Dougherty.

"Joey's grave."

"May we come along?"

Mr. and Mrs. Dougherty agreed.

By then, Doug and I began to worry about an approaching deadline, so we split up. While I returned to the station and logged tape, Doug took his camera to the cemetery and waited at telephoto distance. When the Doughertys appeared, he made a poignant, beautiful shot. On tape, you see the couple arrive, kneel, lay down flowers, and weep. The only sound comes from the blowing wind.

We used that shot to open the piece, along with these words as the family approaches the tombstone:

[TRACK]
IF YOU'RE LUCKY, YOU OBSERVE MEMORIAL DAY
FROM A DISTANCE. YOU HAVE NO CEMETERY TO
VISIT . . . NO LOVED ONE TO REMEMBER. YOU
WOULD NOT BE LIKE GLORIA AND VICTOR
DOUGHERTY, WHO SPENT THIS DAY WITH A
HEADSTONE, AND BLACK-AND-WHITE PICTURES . . .

As the piece develops, we look into the scrapbook and tell an abbreviated version of Joey Artavia's life story. To broaden events at the restaurant, we include sound bites and pictures from some of the other families who were also there. At about the ninety second mark, we resume Joey's story, and return to the opening shot of Mr. and Mrs. Dougherty at the grave:

[TRACK]
SUCH IS THE PAIN OF LOSS . . . OF WONDERING . . .
OF SACRIFICE . . . OF FEELING CHEATED. THIS IS THE
DAY OF NAMES AND FACES . . . OF THOSE WHO
SUFFERED AND PASSED . . . OF THOSE WHO LIVE
ON, AND GROW OLD.

[SOT]
(the wind blows, we pause; Mr. and Mrs. Dougherty
bow their heads)

[TRACK]
. . . IN MEMORY, JOEY ARTAVIA OF MISSION HIGH
SCHOOL, WILL ALWAYS BE NINETEEN . . .

On the timeline, this story begins and ends with our last shot of the day, in the cemetery. The piece worked because we used that one moment to create a structural framework.

## Using Sound Bites to Open or Close a Piece

Once, a colleague and I had a spirited discussion after she opened a story with can't-miss sound of her main character breaking into tears. She reasoned she should use the woman's bite right at the top, before a line of track, because it was the strongest element in her piece.

"It might have worked better later," I suggested to my friend.

"But the woman was absolutely distraught. And we had other strong sound."

"I still think you wasted it at the top."

"Okay. Tell me why."

"Because, without a line of track to set it up, viewers knew nothing about her. How can they care about someone they haven't met yet?"

"The sound bite makes them want to care."

"True, it does get a viewer's attention," I countered. "But the sound bite does little more at that point than objectify her emotion. To make the sound meaningful, I think you needed to introduce her first."

Such are the subjective mysteries of using sound to open or close a television news story. There is no hard-and-fast rule, but here is the guideline I follow: *When you use a sound bite at the beginning or the end of a story, set it up with a line of track.*

In an open, use a preceding line to introduce the moment or the character. In a close, that preceding line of track should signal the story's conclusion; essentially, it's the last line. Any sound that follows should be stronger than any words you might write.

# The Importance of Strong Endings

Speaking of endings, it seems we've neglected them until this point, so now let's give them our full attention. A story's finish is just as, if

not more important than an open. What would any joke be without the punch line? Ever watch an Olympic gymnastic event? Of
what do the announcers remind us? "He needs to nail the landing."

Reporters do, too.

Endings leave the lasting impressions. No matter how strong
the rest of your material may be, a weak ending guarantees a
weak piece. Let's look at some different ways to leave a strong
final impression.

## Refer to the Beginning

In "Rocky's" we found our ending by referring back to the beginning,
with a subtle reference to the opening pictures along Route 66:

> [TRACK]
> . . . AND NYAL ROCKWELL WILL STAY, HE SAYS,
> BECAUSE, AFTER ALL THE YEARS AND ALL THE
> TROUBLES, THIS IS STILL HOME. FOUR HUNDRED
> ACRES, CUT OFF FROM THE HIGHWAY, ON A
> STRETCH OF ROAD NO ONE TRAVELS ANYMORE.

## Ending with Sentiment

In profiles or feature stories, emotion or sentiment almost always
works for endings. We used the technique in a piece about a violin
that once belonged to the great Jascha Heifetz. When he died in
1987, he willed his instrument, known as "the David," to the Fine
Arts Museums of San Francisco, stipulating that it remain in the
city and be played by a worthy musician.

This violin may be the most famous in the world. It comes from
the golden era. Joseph Guarnerius del Gesu, who built the David in
1742, took the secrets of its dark, singular sound to his grave.

The Fine Arts Museums waited several years before deciding on a
recipient. In a quiet backstage practice room during the summer of

2002, curators finally turned over the David to Alexander Barantschik, concertmaster of the San Francisco Symphony Orchestra. As our camera watched, Barantschik opened the case. It looked as if Heifetz had just been there. Barantschik found the violinist's chin piece, some twisted, broken strings, and a few scribbled notes. He was humbled and awestruck. "It's impossible to think that part of his soul is not inside."

As Barantschik tuned the instrument, it came back to life.

"What is the difference between this violin and others?" I asked.

"It has an amazing complexity of sound," said Barantschik. "If you were to compare it with a painting, it has a hundred colors, not fifty. Colors within colors within colors. But it's unforgiving. If you hit the wrong spot, this violin lets you know. And the audience knows. They'll say it used to sound better."

Talk about challenges. Alexander Barantschik received a violin more famous than he—a piece of history that might allow him to create his own. Having spent four years with the London Symphony Orchestra, he already enjoyed world renown, but the David would help him measure it.

Barantschik cradled the instrument as he carried it onto the empty stage of Louise Davies Symphony Hall. He played for himself, for us, for the empty seats, but mostly for the violin. It seemed we were watching the first moments of courtship in an arranged marriage.

In writing the closing line, I pulled information from a sound bite that had been too long to use in the piece. Barantschik's life and work, it seemed, had led to this moment:

> [TRACK]
> WHEN GROWING UP IN RUSSIA, AS THE SON OF A
> FACTORY WORKER, ALEXANDER BARANTSCHIK
> WOULD LISTEN TO MUSIC AS HE WENT TO SLEEP.

THE DAVID IS THE FIRST VIOLIN HE EVER HEARD—
THE ONE THAT ALWAYS PLAYED IN HIS MIND.
NOW, IT'S IN HIS HANDS, AND HE MUST LIVE UP
TO IT.

## Ending with Humor

When appropriate, use humor to wrap a piece—but make certain
it's actually funny. Nothing thuds louder than a dud joke at the end
of a story.

Here's a last line from a piece about an obsessive man who
amassed tens of thousands of miniature liquor bottles, but we left
one fact out until the end. Our character was an alcoholic. He
started collecting only after he quit drinking:

> [TRACK]
> HE GOT HIS LIFE OUT OF THE BOTTLE—
> BUT NOW HE CAN'T GET THE BOTTLES OUT OF HIS
> LIFE.

## Ending with a Twist—Hold a Fact Back

Perhaps you noticed a developing theme in those last two examples. They took what might merely have been additional facts, and
used them as surprise twists. Try the technique when you find
yourself in a storytelling bind. Move your facts around. Save a
strong one for the end.

In 2001, we followed the last door-to-door Fuller Brush salesman, who still made rounds in San Francisco. Norman Hall was
sixty-three years old. Thirty years earlier, he'd begun his career by
peddling sponge mops, air fresheners, and other items to house-
wives in suburban neighborhoods. As you may know, Fuller Brush
salesmen have become an icon of more trusting times, but, as peo-

ple became unwilling to open their doors for strangers, Norman Hall moved his route from suburbia to the less personal world of downtown skyscrapers. Instead of selling door-to-door, he worked floor-to-floor.

"Aren't you something of an anachronism?" I asked him. "Aren't you out of your place and time?"

"I'm Paleolithic," he answered dryly.

We portrayed Norman Hall as a noble, optimistic figure, and the last of a breed. Not many salespeople go cold-calling anymore. Fewer make a living at it. Fuller Brush men went out of style a long time ago, but Norman was the exception—a man who turned sales-manship into a science and, as we hinted, also a performance art.

> [SOT]
> Norman: "I think anything done with flare and brio
> can be artistic . . ."

Until that point in the script, this had been a fairly predictable story, but we'd intentionally saved one factual morsel around which the piece would twist and end. As viewers soon discovered, Norman Hall knew quite a lot about performing because he also worked in local theaters as a character actor. Here's the line that set it up:

> [TRACK]
> CONSIDER THE CONCEPT OF A SALE AS A ONE-ON-
> ONE PERFORMANCE— OF A BOW TIE AS A
> COSTUME . . .

Having turned the corner, we disclosed the rest. When actors go to auditions, they usually begin with an introductory piece from their repertoire. And Norman Hall? He always performed Willy Loman's frustrated soliloquy from *Death of A Salesman*.

At the end of our story, we asked Norman to stand on a busy

sidewalk and recite a few lines. As Willy Loman, Norman was magnificent. He never dropped his sample bag. In that moment, Norman Hall and Willy Loman became one:

> [TRACK]
> THE WORDS WERE PROPHETIC WHEN ARTHUR
> MILLER WROTE THEM. THEY'RE EVEN MORE SO
> TODAY . . .
>
> [SOT]
> Norman as Willie: "There's no such thing as
> friendship anymore. It's all cut-and-dried . . ."
>
> [TRACK]
> IT'S CATALOGUES, IT'S WEB SITES. IT'S EVERYTHING
> NORMAN HALL PUSHES BACK WITH EVERY SALES
> CALL . . .
>
> [SOT]
> Wayne: "WHAT DO WE LOSE WHEN YOU STOP
> SELLING DOOR-TO-DOOR?
>
> Norman: "A fabric of society is gone. A personal
> touch is gone. And it's sad, I think . . ."
>
> [TRACK]
> AS A LAST OF HIS BREED, IT MAKES NORMAN HALL,
> THE DOOR-TO-DOOR SALESMAN, ALL THE MORE
> PRECIOUS.

## Post Script

At the time, Norman Hall's story said quite a lot to me about life,
and a working world in which speed and quantity matter more

than content and quality. Gee. That sounds like our business, sometimes. Our bosses want us to produce segments as quickly and in-
expensively as possible.

Just remember, there can be more to television news storytelling
than the formulated track, sound bite, track, stand-up, methodol-
ogy to which we've grown accustomed. Using structure is a lot like
building a house. Lay a strong foundation on solid ground, and it
will support a variety of forms above.

For reporters, structure provides the most important tool for
writing creatively, even on short notice.

Part II

# PRAGMATICS

# 5

## The Facts of Life in Television News

Here's my definition of the ideal job. Reporters do only the stories they choose. They have the best crews standing by at their personal disposal, ready to roll on a moment's notice. Money is not an issue. Reporters take as long as they like to work on a piece, and as long as they need to tell it.

Dream on.

I made those demands, in jest, to a boss recently. It felt good to get them off my chest. Her response was hysterical, but unprintable.

And now, reality.

The glamour wears off quickly in television news—usually during your first job, when you realize you can't write checks for both the car and the rent in the same pay period. Typically, you will achieve this insight after an unusually exasperating day. What? Jobs in television news can be exasperating?

Absolutely. Every newsroom begins each morning with a blank script, and as many as six hours of live television to fill. Our industry demands speed, but almost always at the cost of perfection. You won't last long in this business if you're a purist. Our bosses don't pay us for doing the flawless story, but for doing the best story possible within limitations. It's only a matter of time until that truth collides with your idealism. In television news, we earn our living by making the best of difficult situations.

## Adapting to Desperate Moments: The Bubble Gum Test

If I ever teach a journalism class, students will have a busy first day. We'll go outside. I'll point at a piece of gum on the sidewalk and give them half an hour to write a story about it.

Here's one possible approach, written from the gum's point of view:

> [TRACK]
> I AM A PIECE OF GUM ON THE SIDEWALK. ONCE I
> LIVED IN A BRIGHT, CLEAN WRAPPER, BUT MY
> OWNER UNFOLDED IT, AND CHEWED ME, AND
> THEN, WITHOUT WARNING OR AN EXPLANATION,
> HE SPIT ME OUT. I'VE BEEN STUCK HERE FOR
> WEEKS NOW. I TURN GOOEY IN THE DAY, AND
> ROCK-HARD AT NIGHT, BUT NO ONE CARES, NOT
> EVEN WHEN I STICK TO THEIR SHOES. THEY JUST
> SCRAPE ME OFF. I DON'T LIKE BEING DISPOSABLE.
> IT HURTS.

Now a second treatment; a mockery of television news at its worst:

> [TRACK]
> WE HAVE LATE-BREAKING NEWS. THERE IS A PIECE
> OF GUM ON THE SIDEWALK, AND IT DOES HAVE
> LOCAL CONNECTIONS. WE DON'T KNOW WHO PUT
> IT THERE, OR WHY, BUT WE'RE HEARING REPORTS
> OF PEOPLE STEPPING ON THIS GUM, AND FOULING
> THEIR CARPETS WITH IT.
> NOW THIS JUST IN. WE'VE LEARNED OF TWO OR
> POSSIBLY THREE MORE PIECES OF GUM NEARBY.
> DETAILS ARE SKETCHY. WE DON'T YET KNOW IF
> THESE NEW PIECES ARE THE SAME FLAVOR, OR
> FROM THE SAME PACK, OR RELATED IN ANY WAY.
> BUT WE CAN CONFIRM AN APPARENT PATTERN,
> AND THE VERY REAL POSSIBILITY OF A SERIAL
> GUM-SPITTER OPERATING IN THE NEIGHBORHOOD.

Don't laugh too hard. Reporters have had to do more with less. Such material would certainly never appear in a newscast, but the exercise has merit. It stands to reason that, if a person can turn a piece of gum into a story, then he probably has the mindset to handle whatever zany challenge comes his way. And it will.

On a reporter's most trying days, equipment will break, or a story won't work out, or the desk will change plans. Without warning, he'll have to scramble and find something else. Successful reporters learn to take aggravating or desperate moments, and adapt.

Two examples come to mind.

## First Day of First Grade

Photographer Johnny Kabasakalis and I still talk about the time we covered a little girl's first day in the first grade. She was the daughter of one of his friends, and she appeared to be a perfect subject.

Johnny spent the night at his buddy's house, and began shooting as soon as the little girl awoke.

All went well until later that morning, when I knocked on the front door. The little girl opened it, took one look at my bald head, and ran away. She wouldn't let me come near her. Still, our producers expected a package. What's a reporter to do? I couldn't exactly call the station and announce, "Sorry, no story. Our little girl thinks I'm the bogeyman."

Johnny saved us with innovative thinking. He suggested that, instead of trying to interview the girl, we use her as a mobile human microphone stand. It made sense. She was only five years old, and she didn't know what a wireless microphone looked like or what it did. Johnny rigged her, kept his distance, and watched her go. That microphone gave us intimate sound and a different kind of piece, written from a child's perspective. If not for the difficulties, we wouldn't have thought to try it.

## The First "Hybrid" Car

In the mid-1980s, General Motors collaborated with Toyota to build a car at a factory in Fremont, California, about forty-five minutes south of San Francisco. Ultimately, that car became the Geo, but, at the time, the companies treated their joint project as top secret. They said only that the new vehicle would combine the best elements of a Chevrolet Nova and a Toyota Corolla.

KRON-TV photographer George Griswold and I went to cover the car's grand debut. Unfortunately, the desk misread the press release and sent us a day early. The security-minded factory wouldn't allow us past the gate, but, when we telephoned the newsroom with our bad news, no one took responsibility. The producers still wanted a piece. "Get reactions or something," they suggested.

Reactions? To what? That left the "or something" part. George and I didn't have a clue what to do, so we drove in circles through the neighborhood, bemoaning our bad luck. Then George noticed an automobile wrecking yard.

"Isn't that an old Corolla?" George asked.

"Isn't that other car a Nova?" I answered.

"Isn't that machine a car crusher?" George continued. We entered the wrecking yard and engaged the owner's sense of humor. Would he use his machine to crush the Nova and Corolla together?

"Sure," he said, and helped us do an irreverent advancer about how the new car might look if the American and Japanese teams didn't work well together.

# A Life in Television News: My Background

I am a middle-aged man living out the career ambitions of a twenty-year-old. At that age, all I wanted was to become a television news reporter. Thirty years later, some of the bloom has faded, but I don't regret a single moment. This can be a wonderful job. It grants a license to pursue your interests, see the world, and ask questions.

Clearly, I love television news reporting enough to obsess about writing this book. Every word comes from the heart, but, given the trend toward bottom lines and deadlines, I'm concerned that narrative storytelling may become impractical or obsolete. It requires a certain amount of time and financial commitment, which not all our corporate masters are willing or able to provide.

## The Speech: "It's Not Like the Good Old Days . . ."

Reporting is a craft that feels more like a calling, but, when we choose this career, most of us don't look at the consequences awaiting us as we grow older. That wide-eyed energy you feel at twenty tends to diminish by fifty. Hopefully, you'll have learned enough by then to work smarter and wiser.

When I was twenty, I had the advantage of having grown up in television. My mother, Alicia Krug Freedman, danced the "Ballet Laurey" role in Agnes DeMille's original Broadway production of *Oklahoma!* She met my father, Mike Freedman, while working on ABC's *Paul Whiteman Revue.*

Dad began with the network in 1948, and later made history as the first photographer to work with a live, handheld electronic camera. He was a "videojournalist" long before anyone came up with the name. He was the first to take pictures on the sideline of a football game; the first to get pictures from the floor of a political convention; the first to carry a live camera into a rodeo pit; the first to go underwater. When, in a 1977 football game against Michigan, Ohio State coach Woody Hayes threw a tantrum after a fumble, he attacked the first person he saw. That was Dad, too, and, yes, he had the shot—live. When Woody slugged Mike Freedman's camera, he also assaulted a national television audience.

"I felt sorry for him," Dad would remark.

Suffice it to say, my pop was a smart guy, and he knew the business. He once told me, "Son, if you want to make a consistent living in television, work in the news. They'll never cancel the news." He was right, as fathers usually are.

Dad dispensed that advice in 1974, the golden age of television news, and by then I'd already caught his journalism bug. Since age fourteen, I'd been writing occasional articles for Los Angeles newspapers. I was in college, and had a full-time, permanent job in the KABC-TV newsroom, cutting and pasting teleprompter copy.

It was there that I decided to become a reporter, but, when I declared those intentions to some of the newsroom veterans, they frowned, shook their heads, and tried to set me straight. "TV news is going to hell," they warned gravely. "It's not like the good old days."

Is anything?

Naturally, their good old days were different from my good old days, which will be different from this generation's good old days—but not that different.

For proof, look no further than a longtime editor in the KGO-TV news department, Elsa Trexler, who keeps a file of directives, complaints, memorandums, and company newsletters. Recently, she shared them with other staff members. These memos were close to thirty years old, but, if you updated the names and looked only at the subject matter, they would be similar to memos of today. True, the technology has changed, but newsrooms, and the personality types working within them, remain more or less the same.

"Has television news gone to hell?" I asked Elsa.

"No more than usual," she smiled.

So now, when young people say they want a life in the business, I make the speech, hoping to save starry-eyed hopefuls from their own glitzy delusions. They listen. They nod as if they understand, but warnings can't substitute for experience. Some will learn the hard way. At best, maybe in another thirty years, those who persevere can warn another generation how television news will be going to hell then, too.

## Darwin

Television news is just as Darwinian as the rest of the world. It seems to conspire against you. The fit adapt and survive.

We work in an industry that caters to people with short attention spans (at least, according to the research). Most news professionals are not proud of that, nor do they happily admit to it, for fear of guilt by association. Quite the contrary—when describing television news to outsiders, we'd prefer to make it sound like brain surgery.

Sorry. It isn't.

## Television News Isn't Just a Living; It's a Lifestyle

If you want to be a television news reporter, expect to pay a price for your success. This is more of a lifestyle than a job. In the first years of your career, you'll become a nomad, moving up to better positions in city after city. You won't starve, but don't expect to earn much more than a basic living wage. Even with an advanced college degree, you'll watch people who never graduated from high school make more money and drive nicer cars and live in bigger houses and have more time off.

Get used to it. The civilians will always have more time off. Many of them will make more money. But television news people have more fun. At least, we did in the good old days.

Accept that television news reporting will inhibit a normal personal life. Expect to feel as if you spend more energy observing other people's problems, struggles, and triumphs than your own.

At times, the job will require twelve-hour days, six or seven days a week, including holidays. If you have a family and work day or evening shifts, plan to miss most of your kid's soccer or Little League games. Forget about coaching. When 6 P.M. comes around, you'll probably be tethered to a live truck instead of relaxing at home. As you get older, this matters.

On a typical day, television news reporters don't have time to sit down and eat a civilized meal. Consequently, we become experts at scarfing lunches in moving cars, sometimes while steering with our knees. We don't chew. We inhale. This is why some of us have terrible table manners.

Our chronic traits include egocentrism, insecurity, self-aggrandizement, and countless other forms of social maladjustment. In short, we're utterly charming, but at least our coworkers help us feel at home. Newsrooms, you see, are like dysfunctional families. We're three-dimensional people stuck in a two-dimensional medium.

If any of this sounds familiar, promise yourself to seek help later.

## Dealing with Management

In any newsroom, reporters must please managers who may change their minds several times a day. Those managers have good intentions, but, inevitably, people make questionable decisions when understaffed and trying to predict the whims of viewers wielding remote controls. "I know it's a little weak," a boss once confided about a story, "but this is one of those days. Just give it the look and feel of news." It's a reporter's job to make even the most wishful of these management decisions look good.

Clearly, reporters and managers do not always agree. While they work together on the same team, they may have different priorities for playing the game. In the field, reporters and crews fight for the quality of their stories. In the newsroom, managers and producers juggle trucks, editors, and overtime to build the best possible broadcast. From this conflict, there will always be tension. Television news is a ratings-oriented industry with sometimes limited resources. As a reporter, you'll be one of them.

## Scavenger Hunts

Television news reporting is like a scavenger hunt. We scramble, hustle, and, at the end of the day, compare our work with that of the competition. If you don't like putting yourself on the line every day, you may be in the wrong business.

In simple terms, being a reporter means performing miracles daily, tirelessly, year after year, for as long as you work, wherever you work, and making those miracles look easy. Brilliance with one story does not does not carry over to the next. You must prove yourself every day. In television newsrooms, institutional equity rarely exists.

## The Right Stuff for Reporters

At twenty years old, I was ignorant of those realities. I blindly assumed I had what it took to be a good reporter, but, if you'd asked for a description of what "it" was, I couldn't have told you. Now, I can.

*Good reporters are curious.* They want to know everything. They learn to find and recognize stories. They can grasp the complexities of issues or events, and then simplify them. Good reporters keep open minds, and present all sides of a story, without bias.

*Good reporters write succinctly, accurately, and emotively.* They understand and apply the principles that make stories work.

*Good reporters manage time.* They meet deadlines and finish stories within prescribed time limits, often with seconds to spare. They write fast. In the most stressful situations, they scribble stories a paragraph and sound bite at a time, handing them off to an editor who cuts them, line by line. It's the equivalent of scaling a cliff without safety ropes.

*Good reporters are researchers and detectives.* They know how and where to locate people. They read those people quickly, gain their trust, ask provocative questions, and elicit memorable answers.

*Good reporters are diplomats.* They negotiate constantly—with management, with crews, with the people in their stories or those who make the people available.

*Good reporters speak clearly, conversationally, spontaneously, and with energy.* Because they do so many live shots, they're equally comfortable when talking to a camera or a person.

*Good reporters develop a specialty.* It may be breaking news, or general assignment, or consumerism, or weather, or features, but they carve niches and rely on them throughout their careers.

*Good reporters find their own voices.* They're confident, with distinctive styles and points of view. Over time, their audiences learn to know them, and to trust them.

*Good reporters learn to alter styles and formats, reflecting the desires of changing management teams.* Don't be surprised when a newsroom's philosophical universe suddenly flips, and what used to be the right way becomes wrong. It's fairly easy to please the boss who hires you. The test is to satisfy that new boss who replaces the old one, while maintaining your self-respect.

## It Takes More Than Good Looks

Contrary to what you might have heard, it takes more than good looks to succeed as a reporter, although good looks certainly help. In most stories, reporters will spend at least 80 percent of the time off camera. More than appearance, long-term survivors rely upon how they sound. As long as a reporter is presentable or memorable, he'll last in the job, provided he masters the other skills first.

Now, if after reading any of this you have reservations about a career in television news reporting, put the rest of this book down, congratulate yourself for exercising good judgment, and back away slowly. Seriously. Enjoy your nice, normal life.

Conversely, if you're willing to be a foot soldier and can't see yourself doing anything else for a living, then keep reading. Welcome to the insane asylum. You just committed yourself.

# 6

## Getting Ahead:
## Create Your Own Luck

In the summer of 2001, baseball star Cal Ripken Jr. made his
farewell retirement tour through every American League city,
and received the royal treatment. Teams declared days in his honor.
They orchestrated gushy ceremonies, bestowing praise and gifts.

Ripken had earned baseball's affection during a sixteen-year
stretch in which he broke Lou Gehrig's supposedly unapproachable
consecutive-game record. Equally important, Ripken did it at a
time when the public perceived professional athletes as spoiled and
overpaid. Because of Ripken's work ethic, average people connected
with him.

For the baseball star, Oakland meant another stop, another

tribute. But, to the local media, it created a whirl of reporters trying to chronicle every step of the great man's last playing visit. As one of those reporters, I knew it would mean a tough day.

Sure enough, when photographer Dave Pera and I arrived at the stadium, we found a Broadway-size cast of radio and television crews already in place, along with public relations people, who established ground rules. "You can take pictures, but no interviews," said one of them. Frankly, reporters have had better access to presidential candidates.

At noon, when Ripken emerged from the dugout, security men formed a protective circle. As he ran down the right field line to stretch, at least a dozen photographers moved with him, running backwards, forwards, and sideways, with those heavy cameras on their shoulders. If one of them had tripped, it would have caused a chain-reaction pileup.

Ripken, meanwhile, ignored their commotion, but not the fans on the first base side of the field. After finishing his warm-ups, he walked toward them. Eager, excited people leaned out, offering memorabilia for him to sign: baseballs, pictures, bats, even themselves. Ripken tried to please everyone. In the midst of a pressing, demanding crowd, he remained humble and gracious, as if this were his first time.

If only the security men had been as accommodating. You'd have thought they were the Secret Service. They kept cameras so far away and blocked so many angles that we couldn't even see Ripken's face. This posed a problem. If we couldn't really see the man and they wouldn't let us interview him, how would we make this piece?

This was one of those times to look the other way. I turned from Ripken, glanced around, and watched his fans. As he passed them in the stands, I noticed how their faces reflected him. You'd have thought the little boys were in the presence of a superhero. And the grown men? They bore the expressions of starstruck boys.

## To Distinguish Your Work, Find an Unusual Angle

To succeed as a reporter, your stories must stand out against the competition. Sometimes, this requires taking a gamble. In sports, they call it having a "heads-up" attitude. Work within the rules, be aware of your surroundings, and anticipate. When you see an opportunity, make the play and do something special.

So, when Ripken and the gaggle moved on, Dave and I hung back and approached fan Herb Saxton, who proudly held a freshly autographed baseball. Saxton was in his twenties, and bore the look of a man who'd just won the lottery, "There is nothing like being here or shaking his hand. No money could buy this. You can't give me five hundred dollars for this right now."

"What does Cal Ripken have that nobody else has?"

"Ripken has dignity," answered Saxton.

It was a start.

### Don't Always Follow the Crowd

At times such as this, my competitive juices take over. It may be a personal fault; it's also a professional strength. The more someone, or an agency, tries to orchestrate news coverage of an event, the more it makes me want to change their "script."

As Ripken moved toward home plate to begin the ceremony, the other crews set their tripods in a semicircle—the pack mentality in action. By playing it safe, they aired similar stories, but missed some telling images.

Dave and I shot the ceremony too, but, instead of locking down in one spot, we moved around. I expected the formal affair would be staid and predictable, and it was, so after getting the requisite pictures we turned away to observe the other ballplayers. In the Athletics dugout, they paid reverential attention. By contrast, Ripken's Orioles teammates exuded boredom. They had seen these tributes before.

"Let's stay on the Orioles side of home plate," I suggested to Dave. This was an intuitive move. Ripken had brought his wife and children along. They stood by, watching. If we couldn't speak with the man himself, I hoped maybe a member of his family would talk, and approached Cal's wife, Kelly.

"No, I don't mind reporters. They're more interested in him," she said, nodding to her husband.

"Would you mind if we ask you a couple of questions on camera?"

"Why not?" Kelly Ripken described Cal as an ordinary guy who never received this kind of superstar treatment at home.

"Does he do the dishes?" I asked.

"No."

After the interview, we stayed nearby. *When you get a good spot, never give it up until someone asks you to leave.* It seemed reasonable that Ripken might pass his wife on his way back to the dugout. We might finally see him up close. Realistically, we couldn't hope for more.

The ceremony ended and Ripken did move toward us. He walked to Kelly and stopped, not two feet away. Just like that, Cal Ripken Jr. and I stood shoulder to shoulder, with nary a security man or any other television crew anywhere nearby. Ripken turned to me and nodded.

"Congratulations," I said like any other fan.

"Thank you," Cal Ripken replied just as casually. We shook

hands, he saw the microphone, and then, in the tone of two guys having an ordinary conversation, I asked a couple of easy questions. The security people looked irritated, but they also knew better than to interrupt Cal Ripken Jr. What he said didn't matter. What did matter is that he said it to us, and only us.

Ripken and I are about the same age and size, but somehow, in reliving the moment, he has grown about six inches taller.

Later, as the game began, a sports reporter from a competing station wandered over. "You lucky dog," he marveled. "You lucky, lucky, lucky dog." Perhaps he's right. Maybe we did luck out. Then again, maybe we *made* our luck, to an extent, by trying to get something different, and then applying a strategy that worked better than expected.

It certainly put me in a positive frame of mind for writing the story:

## CAL RIPKEN'S LAST GAME IN OAKLAND
### August 2001

[TRACK]
(we see Cal Ripken run onto the field as the press
follows)

FOR CAL RIPKEN JR., ROAD TRIPS BRING A
DIFFERENT KIND OF PRESSURE NOW.
HE STILL FEELS IT WITH EVERY MOVE, EVERY STEP,
EVERY BREATH, IN FRONT OF EVERY CROWD IN
EVERY TOWN . . .

[SOT]
Ripken: "It's getting more emotional. I'm thinking of
taking this thing off . . ."

[TRACK]

HE MEANS THE NUMBER EIGHT. IT WAS
EVERYWHERE AT THE COLISEUM TODAY.
ON BASES . . .
IN BATTING CIRCLES . . .
ON PHOTOS . . .
THERE HAS BEEN A CAL RIPKEN DAY IN EVERY
AMERICAN LEAGUE CITY IN THIS, HIS FAREWELL
SEASON, AND HIS WIFE KELLY HAS BEEN THERE FOR
EVERY ONE OF THEM . . .

[SOT]

Wayne asks Kelly: "IS HE AS PERFECT AS HE
SEEMS?"

Kelly: "I don't know anyone who's perfect."

Wayne: "DOES HE DO THE DISHES?"

Kelly: "No."

[TRACK]

BUT, AS A BASEBALL PLAYER AND MERE MORTAL,
CAL RIPKEN SET HIMSELF APART BY PLAYING IN
2,632 STRAIGHT GAMES.
FOR SIXTEEN YEARS BEGINNING IN 1982, HE NEVER
MISSED A DAY OF WORK . . .
NEVER COPPED AN ATTITUDE . . .
NEVER CHANGED TEAMS . . .

[STAND-UP]

THE STREAK ENDED IN 1998, AND, IN THE TIME
SINCE, ITS LEGEND HAS GROWN. WHEN PEOPLE
TALK ABOUT CAL RIPKEN, THEY USE WORDS LIKE
CONSISTENCY. . .
LONGEVITY . . .

LOYALTY . . .
HE NEVER TOOK THE JOB, OR THE GAME, FOR
GRANTED.

[SOT]
Wayne: "WHAT DO YOU THINK THESE FANS SEE IN
YOU?"

Ripken: "Someone who loves the game. Who does
his best, I suppose . . ."

[TRACK]
AND SO, BEFORE TODAY'S GAME, CAL RIPKEN
SPENT A FEW MINUTES GIVING LIFETIME MEMORIES
TO SOME OF THE PEOPLE WHO IDOLIZE HIM.
WATCH THEIR FACES.
YOUNG BOYS SAW HIM AS A SUPERHERO.
GROWN MEN FELT LIKE YOUNGSTERS AGAIN.
AMONG THEM, HERB SAXTON, WHO HELD A BALL
RIPKEN HAD JUST SIGNED.

[SOT]
Herb Saxton, a fan: "There is nothing like being here
or shaking his hand. No money could buy this. You
can't give me five hundred dollars for this right
now."

Wayne: "WHAT DOES CAL RIPKEN HAVE THAT
NOBODY ELSE HAS?"

Herb: "Ripken has dignity."

[TRACK]
DIGNITY—A SIMPLE DESCRIPTION WE DON'T OFTEN
HEAR ABOUT PRO ATHLETES ANYMORE.

BUT, IN OAKLAND TODAY, IT FIT . . . TO SAY CAL
RIPKEN JR. HAS DIGNITY MAY BE THE BIGGEST
TRIBUTE OF THEM ALL.

## Cream Rises

Television news people can be a jealous, petty lot. Out of frustration or insecurity they belittle their competition, and even their colleagues.

"How did he get that job?"

"How did she get that story?"

"Can you believe the luck of that guy?"

But, in television news, luck is not entirely accidental. If, early in my career, someone offered a chance to be either lucky or good, I would have chosen the former. Now, I know better. Luck helps most when you've prepared to take advantage of it.

It reminds me of the first time my father took me fishing. Being a typical kid, I spent most of my energy baiting the hook and casting the line. Meantime, Dad caught all the fish. This didn't make sense. I was working harder.

"Nobody ever caught a fish without his hook in the water," Dad said. "Fisherman's luck has a lot to do with knowing where the fish might be, and then keeping your hook wet."

Extend the metaphor, and you'll find this theory also applies to life. Television news is no exception.

## Local Knowledge

On November 12, 2002, Iraq's parliament rejected a United Nations weapons inspections resolution, pushing us closer to war. That day, KGO-TV's assignment desk received a tip that former president Bill Clinton was playing a round of golf at San Francisco's Olympic

Club. Our assistant news director, Tracey Watkowski, broke me off another assignment to track him down. We were hoping Clinton would comment on the situation.

The Olympic Club is an exclusively private establishment. When we telephoned and asked for admittance, the head professional politely referred us to the general manager, who was "unavailable," according to his office. So, instead of trying to get information from the highest levels, I went in below the radar and called the desk in the pro shop, where assistants answer the phone.

"I hear Clinton already teed off," I prompted the kid who picked up.

"Sure did," he volunteered. "Nine forty-five on the Lake course."

This meant Clinton had been golfing for almost three hours. I calculated he would be approaching the tenth or eleventh hole by then. Having played Olympic, I knew the thirteenth runs along the course's edge next to a chainlink fence. On the other side are a creek and, past some woods, a road.

Photographer Doug Laughlin and I parked our truck, slashed through the bushes, and waited. A few minutes later, two Secret Service men appeared, followed by the former president's foursome. Mr. Clinton looked surprised to see us, but waved.

We waved back.

Clinton finished the hole and we shouted for him to come over. "Sir, how about a word with a couple of bushwhackers?"

He laughed at the pun, walked twenty-five feet out of his way down a bank, and answered a question about Iraq. "President Hussein was always homicidal, but not suicidal," said the ex-president. "I hope there won't be a conflict, but if he doesn't let the inspectors in there will be."

Clinton delivered that statement through the fence and over a creek, but Doug and I didn't care. It made the day, the week, and the month. We scored an exclusive one-on-one with a former president who then moved to the next tee, hit a bad shot, and took a mulligan.

Yes, we saw that through the clearing, too.

## CLINTON IN THE WOODS
### November 2002

[TRACK]
IT'S NOT EVERY DAY THAT FORMER PRESIDENT BILL
CLINTON COMES TO TOWN . . . AND EVEN LESS
LIKELY THAT HE'LL INVITE REPORTERS TO WATCH
HIM PLAY GOLF.

[SOT]
(swings)

[TRACK]
AS USUAL, THE SECRET SERVICE PROTECTED HIM . . .
AS EXPECTED, COURSE MANAGEMENT KEPT THE
PRESS OFF ITS PROPERTY.
BUT THERE IS A CLEARING BY THE FENCE ALONG
THE THIRTEENTH HOLE . . .

[SOT]
Wayne: "SIR . . . HOW ABOUT A WORD . . ."

[TRACK]
. . . ON A MORNING WHEN THE FORMER
PRESIDENT CLEARLY WANTED TO RELAX, HE LEFT
HIS FOURSOME TO COMMENT ON THE IRAQI
PARLIAMENT'S REJECTION OF THE UNITED NATIONS
WEAPONS INSPECTIONS RESOLUTION . . .

[SOT]
Clinton: "Well, now they're asking for a conflict.
The inevitable conclusion is they have chemical and
biological weapons and they don't want to give up."

[TRACK]
BASED ON THAT RESPONSE, MR. CLINTON APPEARS
TO BE AS KEENLY INTERESTED IN WORLD AFFAIRS
AS EVER.
WHEN ASKED TO TRANSLATE THE LANGUAGE OF
DIPLOMACY, CLINTON SOUNDED LIKE A
STATESMAN, NOT A POLITICIAN.

[SOT]
Clinton: "My guess is they're still playing games. I
cannot believe they really want a conflict because
before, President Hussein was always homicidal,
but not suicidal. I hope there won't be a conflict,
but if he doesn't let the inspectors in there will
be."

[TRACK]
SUCH IS THE LIFE OF A FORMER PRESIDENT.
FROM A PRIVATE CITIZEN, TO A PLAYER ON THE
WORLD STAGE, AND THEN BACK TO GOLF . . . ALL
IN TWO MINUTES.

As a reporter in any market, you can apply such local knowledge
to the job every day. Do you know the radio frequencies of your
local fire department, police, and airport? Do you have good working relationships with the people who run them? Do you have a reliable reputation overall? People speak to, and take chances with,
reporters they trust.

At the scene of a murder, do you know the detectives by sight and name? Are you familiar with the routines and protocols of an investigation? If so, you'll also recognize when police will remove the body. If you've worked with the coroner before, he might tell you his exit route in advance. With such information, you can place your camera to get just the right angle. (I am not a fan of such visuals in a newscast, but at times they're necessary.)

After finishing a piece, do you file information in a computer? Do you cross-reference names, telephone numbers, job descriptions, and areas of expertise? After a few months, the data adds up.

How many telephone calls do you make to sources? If you made one extra call a day, they would total five in a week. With that many hooks in the water, you have a good chance of catching something.

## Set Your Own Standards

When evaluating your performance, be your own best critic. Set higher standards for yourself than those of your competitors and coworkers.

In your first job, especially, don't worry too much about days off, vacations, and setting down roots. You'll never again learn so much about your craft in such a short period of time. If you aren't excited about going to work every day, regardless of the hours, consider another career.

As in any field, it takes a dedicated effort to improve. Find reporters you admire. Study their stories. Model your own pieces to reflect your career aspirations. Your reel should look like, and have the quality of, the place you want to go, not the one in which you work.

If, at the end of a day, you made mistakes with a piece, or ran out of time and couldn't finish it the way you wanted, return to the edit room and get it right. You aren't as likely to repeat errors when you correct them.

## Learn to Love the Process

People go into television news for many reasons—excitement, commitment, vanity, and fame, among others. But the ones who last usually say they've learned to love the process. On bad days, the process gets them through.

Even if you don't like an assignment, always give it your best effort. That's part of the process. Your weakest stories will reveal as much about you as your best.

If life is about the journey, reporting is about the doing. Commit to high standards in every phase of a piece, from making the phone calls, to asking the right questions, to logging the tape, to writing the script, to voicing the copy, to scrutinizing the edits. One or two frames, pictures, facts, words, or phrases can make a career's worth of difference.

That's the process.

This is a philosophy. Fishermen, too, follow a process when they cast their lines. Why else would they call it fishing instead of catching?

# The Right Place at an Unfortunate Time: "On the Street, Lost and Forgotten"

In 1982, KRON-TV's managing editor, Doug Caldwell, took a risk with photographer Todd Hanks, editor George Griswold, and me. We were new to the staff, but he assigned us a series about homelessness on San Francisco's streets. Why Todd? Why George? Why me? Maybe he figured we were young, single, and hungry enough to regard working all night as fun.

We threw ourselves into the project, and linked up with a group of city-roaming winos who became recurring central characters in the stories. Their unofficial spokesman was a scruffy guy they called Rubidub, who earned the name "because I used to drink rubbing alcohol. Whenever we open a new bottle, we always pour a little out for the brothers."

"The brothers?"

"Yeah," continued his buddy, Norman Bushard. "We toast the brothers who died in the war and on the streets and in the penitentiary." Norman spoke in a thick working-class accent and always wore a soiled navy blue stocking cap. He had a weepy left eye. From that side of his face, he always appeared to be crying, but, from the right, he looked scowling and mean.

Rubidub, legally named Robert Brennan, had fought in Vietnam. He wore a full beard with matted, shoulder-length hair, and saw the world through a pair of large, cracked glasses held together by a thick wad of surgical tape. He looked half-blind and completely deranged. "After the divorce, I hit the streets, " he explained. "It's the life I want to lead. It's freedom."

It only took a whiff to notice that Rubidub rarely bathed. There must have been six years of dirt caked into the folds of his neck. You've never met a louder, more obnoxious, and sometimes articulate drunk, nor would you want to.

Todd, George, and I spent so many days and nights with these men that we began to wonder if we were covering this story or becoming part of it. We watched the winos get arrested and, just as quickly, released. San Francisco didn't have an effective system for dealing with its drunken homeless, and they, in turn, couldn't plan beyond their next bottle. The gang slept in bushes and under freeways, and proclaimed their lifestyle to be grand.

It took us two weeks to produce three long pieces, but, with only one more day to shoot, "On the Street: Lost and Forgotten," as we called it, still needed an ending. Todd, George, and I thought about watching a homeless person's funeral at sea, but there wasn't one scheduled.

Since nobody had a better idea, Todd suggested another visit to the Tenderloin district, where we'd spent most of our time. Maybe we would run across Rubidub and Norman, and could ask about the end of their cycle.

Did they realize it led to an abyss?

But, for once, as Todd, George, and I drove through the neighborhood, we couldn't find the winos. They'd disappeared. Hours passed. As sunset approached, we began to lose hope. "It's not happening," said Todd.

"Let's keep trying," I insisted. Keep that hook in the water.

Out of desperation, I threw up a wild prayer. "Help us find an ending."

We parked and tried to formulate a plan. Then, when we least expected it, we either got lucky, or else received divine intervention. Rubidub, Norman, and maybe ten members of their gang walked around the corner and greeted us. They were cold sober, for once, and able to speak rationally.

We told them what we wanted, and rolled tape. "Do you worry about dying?" I asked Bushard.

"No, no, no. I don't care. I don't care about dying at all," he said bitterly. Bushard and the others talked tough, defending their drinking and their homeless lifestyle.

Rubidub, soft-spoken and sensitive in sobriety, described the wife, kids, and mortgage he'd left behind. "If I die right now, so be it. That's dead and stinkin', man. Nobody gets out of life alive."

We recorded forty minutes of such bold talk. When I ran out of questions, Todd asked a few more. As a reporter, I never had a problem with that, nor he with my framing an occasional shot. Todd, George, and I worked collaboratively, as a team. We shared ideas in the field, in the writing, and also when editing. This project belonged to all of us.

Todd must have asked the guys six or seven questions. Whatever the number, he kept us there long enough to witness a sad but extraordinary climax to our weeks on the street.

Earlier in the conversation, a wino named Melvin Schmidt had gotten up and stumbled away. At the time, we didn't pay much notice. Schmitty, as they called him, was the old man of the group and had been barely coherent in interviews. "I'm down for the count," he once told us on camera.

That statement would be prophetic.

We ended our heart-to-heart with the winos only after Todd's camera battery ran low. But then, as we thanked the gang and began packing up, an ambulance approached with siren blaring, and stopped just around the corner. There we found Schmitty, staring at the sky, dead, with an empty bottle of Night Train wine in his hand.

Todd squeezed just enough juice from his battery to record the winos as they saw Schmitty and broke into tears. Five minutes earlier, these same guys had spoken boldly about defying death. Strange how, while they did so, death made its own play just a few steps away.

"Dammit! Oh, Schmitty, man, please don't go," pleaded Buschard. Todd kept rolling tape, hoping the battery would last a little longer. Thankfully, we'd brought along a radio, and George used it to make a frantic call for fresh batteries. KRON-TV photographer Chuck Hastings heard us from two blocks away and came to our rescue.

It was another of many breaks that day, but, in retrospect, we captured this remarkable scene because earlier, when our prospects for finding the story seemed most bleak, we stayed with it.

I cannot explain why all this happened then, and in front of a camera. Luck, certainly, had nothing to do with it. Schmitty would have died whether we'd been there or not. Still, it was upsetting to watch and difficult to report. I'm probably trite and self-absorbed in believing his death served a greater purpose, but it feels better that way.

Or maybe Rubidub summed up the event more succinctly with this comment: "At least he died drunk."

# 7

When You Have No Time: Hamburger Helpers for Television News

Perhaps you've seen *Iron Chef*, a Japanese television show in which two culinary masters, a champion and a challenger, have one hour in which to create gourmet meals from identical but limited ingredients.

"Why do you like this show?" my wife once asked.

"Because I do the same thing."

"But you hardly cook."

True, but as television reporters we can relate to those chefs and their challenges because we are their short-order journalistic equivalents. Like the Iron Chefs, reporters work with limited ingredients and tight deadlines, and almost always deliver.

Let's be realistic about the job. Most major-market stations cover large geographic areas with a relatively small number of crews. Reporters may wait several hours for an available camera, and commonly spend more time driving to and from an assignment than shooting or editing. Such conditions turn crews into quick-strike teams, traveling fast and light.

The next time you find yourself in a hurry, try a few of the following suggestions. If you can't be the Iron Chef, become the Iron Reporter.

## Humanize

How often have you heard someone described like this in a story?

> [TRACK]
> MABEL THORPE HAS WORKED IN THIS POTATO CHIP
> FACTORY FOR THE LAST TWENTY YEARS . . .

How much does that line really tell you about her? And yet, many reporters automatically use age or years to characterize someone, overlooking how just one more thoughtfully chosen fact might add substance and depth:

> [TRACK]
> . . . THAT'S A LONG TIME TO WATCH CHIPS ON A
> CONVEYOR BELT, BUT MABEL NEVER SAW THE JOB
> THAT WAY BECAUSE, BY SITTING HERE, SHE SAVED
> ENOUGH MONEY TO PUT A SON THROUGH MEDICAL
> SCHOOL . . .

And now you know Mabel better. When she speaks, you know where she's coming from, and her words carry more weight.

# Find the Details; Write Outside the Corners of the Frame

Mabel's son is an example of how, even when you don't have perfect sounds or pictures, you can expand a story by writing outside of the frame. Make the piece bigger by adding small details.

Read the work of Edna Buchanan, whose crime reporting for the *Miami Herald* won her a Pulitzer Prize for general news reporting in 1986. She's the queen of details. In her book *The Corpse Had a Familiar Face,* Buchanan describes how, if a wife killed her husband while he watched television, she'll go so far as to ask the name of the program:

> Police say she bludgeoned her husband to death with a frying
> pan as he sat in an easy chair in the living room. The tv was on
> channel 5. It was 7:15 p.m. He had been watching *Family Feud.*

Those kinds of details—the frying pan, the time, the channel, and the show—give texture to the story. Edna Buchanan could never know enough. She'd ask what a deceased was wearing, and even what the coroner found in his pockets. Such small pieces of information bring dead people back to life, at least in print.

Details can work the same way in television news stories, particularly when you don't have time to shoot, or time to tell.

## Richmond Explosion

In 1999, a plastics recycling company blew up in Richmond, California, north of San Francisco. The blast spewed debris and toxic fumes downwind. Here's the first line of that piece. I wrote both inside and outside the frame by describing not only what I saw, but also what I smelled and heard:

[TRACK]
EVEN WITHOUT THE RAIN, RICHMOND STREETS
WOULD HAVE BEEN EMPTY THIS MORNING.
IT TOOK ONLY ONE LOOK AT THE RISING SMOKE . . .
ONE ACRID WHIFF AND THE SOUND OF
HELICOPTERS. . . .
IT TOOK ONLY ONE OR TWO PIECES OF BURNED
PLASTIC.
THEY CLUNG TO THE TELEPHONE LINES AND
FLUTTERED DOWN LIKE FALLOUT FROM A POLYMER-
FILLED SKY.

From the start, this was a hectic morning. The station dispatched crews from everywhere, or so it seemed. As soon as I linked up with photographer Ron Guintini, the assignment desk ordered us to find a local resident, any resident, and to tell his or her story. We picked the first person we saw, Gleena Allen, a single mother of three. She'd been sitting in a parked car with the windows rolled up, and agreed to let us follow her home:

[TRACK]
. . . TO THE HOUSE SHE GREW UP IN, JUST TWO
BLOCKS DOWNWIND FROM THE EXPLOSION . . .

There, Gleena introduced us to her children and then to her hunchbacked seventy-six-year-old grandmother, Willie, who barely looked up while frying salt pork on the kitchen stove. She told us she suffered from heart and lung problems. The explosion made her feel worse. "I smell it here inside this house," she said. "Can't hardly breathe."

"Can you describe the smell?"

"It's like a knife handle burning on a stove."

From there, we moved to the living room and asked the oldest daughter, Leticia, about her experience with the explosion. "It shook the whole house, like an earthquake," she told us.

Fifteen minutes later, the family packed up their car and left, but by then we'd gathered good details to use in my narrative track:

> [TRACK]
> BY ELEVEN A.M. THE FAMILY DECIDED THEY'D HAD
> ENOUGH . . .
>
> [SOT]
> Gleena tells kids: "Get your shoes; we're out of
> here."
>
> [TRACK]
> THEY LEFT THE SALT PORK SITTING ON THE STOVE.
> THEY LEFT THE DISHES IN THE SINK.
> THEY LEFT THE HOUSE AND TOOK OFF FOR
> CLEANER AIR AT AUNT VERNA'S HOUSE. BUT AUNT
> VERNA LIVES JUST TWO MILES AWAY . . .

## Change the Scene

From start to finish, the piece took less than one hour to shoot, but, by showing several different locations, including the street, the house, and Aunt Verna's place, we made it visually interesting. At each of those locations, Ron Guintini layered in more details.

On the street, he shot the sky, the power lines, and the family car. In the house he shot the salt pork in the frying pan, dirty dishes in the sink, and latched windows in the living room. At Aunt Verna's, he took pictures from outside and inside the apartment.

The piece never repeats a scene. By visiting so many places and showing so many elements, the story moved like lightning, even at more than two and a half minutes.

## Use Tape Wisely

When working with multiple locations, the key is not to overshoot. You shouldn't need more than sixty seconds of raw video from any one place, unless you plan to dwell there in the piece. Sometimes, one long shot will do—just enough to set up natural sound or a sound bite.

Keep those interviews short and to the point. Discipline yourself to know what you want, get it, and move on. By shooting in short bursts, you'll save precious time in screening, writing, and editing.

This technique works just as effectively in any kind of story, whether breaking news, general news, or a feature.

# Use Pictures and File Video to Expand the Time Frame

When someone pulls a photograph from his wallet and shows it to you, don't you learn more about the person? Reporters achieve the same effect by using photographs in television news stories. Pictures show how a subject has aged or changed. They expand the time frame. Home movies and file video work the same way.

Once, we faced a short deadline while doing a story about Carla Picci, a teenage girl struck by lightning in her right arm. After a brief hospital stay, doctors sent her home where, like a typical sixteen-year-old, she worried only about tryouts for the softball team, three days hence. "I want to make the squad," she told us, "but my arm hurts."

How could we visualize that? Carla found a photograph of herself posing in a softball uniform. We stuck it to the refrigerator, rolled a few seconds of video, and used it in the piece. No, this wasn't the same as seeing Carla actually play, but it did provide a visual reference, and showed her in another setting.

## Change the Background During Interviews

In the early 1990s, Yuba City, California, earned *Money* magazine's distinction of being America's worst place to live. The day of the announcement, KGO-TV chartered a plane and sent us north, but unfortunately we got a late start. After landing, renting a car, and driving into town, we had all of thirty minutes in which to shoot the story and return to the airport, so we made the most of what we could get. For our wide shot of the town, we used an aerial from the plane. Later, we pointed our camera out the car window for driving shots down the main street.

But thirty minutes to shoot—that's cutting it close, and we still needed reactions from local citizens. As time ticked away, we stopped outside a shopping center, and grabbed interviews in the parking lot, but from what viewers saw we might as well have spoken with people in four different locations.

How? North, south, east, and west. The four directions presented four different views. From that parking lot we could see the shopping center, the mountains, the main street through town, and a stand of trees. *By facing people in different directions, we changed the backgrounds.*

Even when not in a hurry, I routinely use that technique. It's just good television. If you know you'll need more than one sound bite from a person, rotate or move him during casual interviews. By altering the background even slightly, you subtly change the scene and keep the visuals more interesting.

## Change the Light and Camera Angles

In the early 1990s, KGO-TV newsroom staff members began receiving yellow three-by-five cards in the mail from Leon Lukaszewski, one of our viewers. His messages politely but firmly corrected our grammar. "Your copy in the segment April 8 suffered from an elementary case of singular, plural conflict," Lukaszewski once wrote.

Who was this guy?

I made a call and learned that our self-appointed grammar policeman had retired after twenty-three years of copyediting the *Los Angeles Times*. But once an editor, always an editor. Lukaszewski couldn't let it alone, and took it out on the media. When he watched television, he kept a pencil and paper in his hand, intending to prevent what he called contagious diseases of the English language. "What happens is some moron comes up with an expression," said Lukaszewski. "And I wonder how he can get away with it. And soon everyone else in town is getting away with it."

Leon Lukaszewski made a wonderful character.

But his story would challenge us because most of it took place in one small room of his house. Thankfully, photographer Cathy Cavey is an expert at working with light and angles. She made the piece work. First, she took the camera outside, and shot Lukaszewski through a window.

Once inside, Cavey used the natural light coming in through that same window, then the fluorescent light on his desk, and, later, she bounced her own tungsten light off a wall. She even turned the room lights off when Mr. Lukaszewski watched television. Cathy knows how light varies in texture and so, accordingly, does its look.

Additionally, she changed the physical level of the camera, shooting high, low, around doorways, and through openings.

In actual size, Leon Lukaszewski's room might have been ten by twelve feet. But, by the time Cathy Cavey finished shooting, she'd made it look three times bigger.

## The Theory in Practice: Hard News in a Hurry

We used several of these hurry-up techniques while covering the remnants of a forest fire in northern California. Photographer Clyde Powell and I were supposed to fly in by helicopter, shoot a few pictures, and then do two quick live shots with voiceovers and sound bites. The assignment editor told us specifically, "Don't bother with a package."

We arrived in the fire zone with just enough time to visit the Red Cross shelter. There, we interviewed a woman who had lost her house in the fire. She told how her son and daughter, who lived two doors away, had also lost their homes. "It just wiped our family out," said the woman.

As it turned out, those houses lay between us and our live-shot location. We stopped en route, took pictures, and used them, along with her interview, during the live shots.

Except for the helicopter ride, it had been a simple day, but as we headed for home my pager chirped, displaying a message to call the desk. Usually, this does not portend good news.

"Your satellite window is at 9:00," the assignment editor said. "Keep the package to less than two minutes."

"What window? What package? Nobody said anything about a package." Not to us, anyway. But the station had hired a new and zealous producer for the late broadcast, and he wanted an update on the fire. Nothing would dissuade him, even after we explained how both the flames and sun had almost disappeared behind opposite mountain ridges. The producer didn't care. He'd created a slot in his rundown and he expected us to fill it.

## Be the Solution, Not the Problem

Both Clyde and I had been in the business long enough to know that it rarely pays to fight the desk. Save the energy for the assignment. Be a solution, not a problem.

We sat down on a couple of tree stumps, shook our heads, and muttered some unprintable words. We hadn't a clue about what to do.

About five minutes later a couple of minivans, packed with kids and belongings, pulled up. An exhausted-looking woman, Lynn Doro, slammed a door and trudged toward us. "Do you know the way to Buzzard's Roost?" she asked.

"No," I answered. "But would you like to be on television?"

Examine my reasoning. Lynn Doro was somehow involved with the fire. If we couldn't cover the big story, at least we could tell a small one about her, and that would be enough.

In Lynn's case, she just wanted to get home. "On the day of the fire, as we left our house at Buzzard's Roost, the flames were moving as fast as our car was." After four days of running, and with the roads still closed, she and her husband, Bill, wanted to find a back way in. "I was told we can't cut through. But maybe we can use our knowledge of the back roads," Bill hoped.

Lynn gave us an interview at that first location. Then she and her family climbed back into their minivans to see if a roadblock had opened. Clyde hauled his gear into one of the vans and rode with them. The Doros didn't travel more than a mile, but, by using a ten-second shot inside the vehicle, Clyde gave viewers a sense of sharing space, spending time, and journeying with them. It gave the piece a feeling of intimacy.

When the family stopped again at the roadblock, we took more pictures and asked more questions. Now we'd seen them in two locations and had the beginnings of a narrative.

But what next? How could we expand the story's scope? Well, we had that interview with the woman from the Red Cross center. And what about those burned homes? We used both those elements in the middle of the piece, adding overview and depth.

To close the piece, we returned to the Doro family pulling into a third location, a campground, where they would spend another night away from home. In total, Clyde and I spent less than half an hour with them, but the package ran two minutes, using ten minutes of raw tape from six locations.

Better yet, we'd cobbled together enough ingredients for a narrative story: a beginning, a middle, an ending, main characters, and a quest.

## THE FOUNTAIN FIRE
### September 1992

[TRACK]
WE MET HER DURING ONE OF THOSE IN-BETWEEN
PERIODS. WITH THE SUN FALLING BEHIND ONE
RIDGELINE AND A HOTSPOT RISING ON THE OTHER,
LYNN DORO WANTED TO GET HER FAMILY HOME
AFTER THREE DAYS OF RUNNING.

[SOT]
Lynn: "On the day of the fire, as we left our house
at Buzzard's Roost, the flames were moving as fast
as our car was . . ."

[TRACK]
AND, TONIGHT, THEY'RE STILL MOVING, TRYING TO

GET HOME. SO HUSBAND BILL TOOK THE DOGS IN
ONE VAN. LYNN CARRIED THE KIDS IN ANOTHER, AS
THEY TRIED TO FIND A WAY THROUGH THE FIRE
ZONE. INSTEAD, THEY HIT ONE ROADBLOCK AFTER
ANOTHER.

[SOT]
Bill: "I was told we can't cut through. But maybe we
can use our knowledge of the back roads to find a
way in now."

[TRACK]
IT HAS BEEN THIS WAY FOR MANY LOCAL FAMILIES.
WHEN THE FOUNTAIN FIRE BROKE OUT LAST
THURSDAY, PEOPLE GRABBED WHAT THEY COULD.
THEY'VE BEEN MOVING EVER SINCE. AND YET, BY
SOME STANDARDS, THE DOROS ARE LUCKY. THE
FOUNTAIN FIRE HAS DESTROYED 308 HOMES SO
FAR. IT'S FILLED EVACUATION CENTERS WITH WIPED-
OUT FAMILIES.

[SOT]
Woman in the Red Cross center: "When the fire
came through, it just wiped our family out. It got
me, my son, my daughter. Everything's gone."

[SOT]
(doors slam as we see Lynn and Bill climb out of
their cars again, now in a parking lot)

[TRACK]
WHEN WE SAID GOODBYE TO LYNN AND BILL
TONIGHT, THEY WERE STILL IN LIMBO. THE LAST

THEY HEARD, THEIR HOUSE STILL STOOD, BUT
THERE WERE FLAMES IN THE AREA.
GOOD NEWS . . .
BAD NEWS . . .
NO NEWS, REALLY . . .

[SOT]
Lynn: "This is like being chased. I feel as if I've been chased by this fire since an hour after it started."

Bill: "This is four days now. Four days of not sleeping through the night . . ."

Lynn: "Maybe we should find a motel and get some rest."

Bill: "Yeah, a bath and shower would be good. Then maybe we can go to a movie and forget about all this until tomorrow, when we'll try it all again."

# Post Script:
# Television News Versus Orthodontics

An intern in our newsroom stopped by for a chat recently. She'd just turned down a scholarship and career in orthodontics to pursue reporting. "Are you sure you want to do that?" I asked. As an orthodontist, each of her projects would last a lifetime, not ninety seconds. Better still, patients would expect her to do the best possible job, without taking shortcuts. "Don't you see the luxury in that? Television news, while well-intentioned, cannot approach that standard."

"Teeth bore me," said the intern.

Television news reporting will always involve compromise, to a degree, but that doesn't mean we have to sell out in making it. Quite the contrary; knowing the ideal sets a standard. By seeing what a story lacks, you may be able to make up for it some other way. "But don't let the ideal stand in the way of the good," I told the intern. "If that bothers you . . ."

She finished my sentence: ". . . then become an orthodontist."

# 8

## Thread Stories
## Around Spontaneous Moments

If aliens visited Earth and landed among the tailgate parties before an Oakland Raiders home game, they would take one look,
run back to their space ship, and never return.

"Earthlings are menacing and dangerous," the aliens might report. They would have found themselves among goblins, ghouls,
and monsters, all dressed in silver and black—a beer-frothing,
meat-eating, garlic-spewing mob. No doubt, every professional
football team has its own cadre of devoted, bizarre fans, but for
sheer spectacle nothing compares with the costumed, maniacal
misfits of the Raider Nation.

For years, its citizens have gathered in tribelike clans. They've staked out territories in the Coliseum's massive parking lot, and there they have convened. No one has ever drawn official boundaries or markings, but among Oakland Raider fans, these sacred sections of concrete turf are known and respected.

"Yeah, like this is our light pole," Raider fan Rick Sanders once showed me. "D-24. That's us."

At least, it used to be. In the fall of 2001, Network Associates Coliseum managers traded anarchy for revenue, and changed the parking policy. They resurfaced the lot and repainted the lines into smaller spaces. Where before, fans could park anywhere, the new system removed free choice and funneled cars into sections. "It's a matter of safety and efficiency," explained a Coliseum spokeswoman.

"They want us to be sheep," Sanders countered. "I'm mad. I'm teed off."

He wasn't alone. In the weeks leading up to the first preseason home game, the war of words escalated. Coliseum management wouldn't back down, nor would Raider fans, who threatened blatant disobedience.

Local news stories don't get much better than this.

On game day, cars lined up hours in advance. Some of them came in convoys, hoping to break the rules and park together in their usual places, but, when the lots opened, they never had the chance. Coliseum parking attendants waved flags, blew whistles, and herded them, like cattle, through a series of metal gates into tight little compliant rows.

Raider fans, who pride themselves on their renegade image, took this as the ultimate insult. "I can't stand it," whined one of them, Rick Borba. We found him in the parking lot, standing with crossed arms and a defiant look on his face, guarding his old spot. After six seasons of barbecuing there, Borba still clung to impossible hopes for a rendezvous. "We're loyal fans, and this is how they treat us?"

After the interview, photographer Jack Fraser took a few more pictures of Borba. While tape rolled, another man came running. His approach ruined Fraser's sequence, but the photographer had the good sense to keep shooting as the newcomer breathlessly shouted, "Rick, you got a casualty. Your wife just hit a car." He still wore the microphone, so we followed as he investigated the damage.

Sure enough, a Coliseum attendant had taken his directives a little too seriously, and ordered Mrs. Borba to pull into a space already occupied by another car's open door. She was now furious, explaining how the attendant had insisted she move into the space. "I told him I didn't want to ruin that car's door, but he made me pull forward. He made me drive into it."

Mrs. Borba spoke with passionate animation. We could have stopped her to pin a microphone, but that would have interrupted the moment. Instead, Jack sacrificed some sound quality by using the microphone on top of his camera. Whatever we might have lost in clarity, we more than made up with spontaneity.

Next we heard from David DeLoach, who owned the car Mrs. Borba had hit. He gestured to the frazzled attendant and told us a similar story. "He told the lady to pull up. She didn't want to. He insisted, and then she ran into my door."

It was only a small dent—hardly serious damage, but it served as a catalyst in uniting all parties against Coliseum management. This was the stuff of news on a serving plate—a minor drama amid the bigger one. If on good days you'll identify a main character, then on the better ones you'll also find a narrative thread to weave through the story.

We followed up by interviewing Mark Kaufman, the Coliseum's general manager, who defended his new policy. Lastly, we took a few more pictures of other cars in the parking lot. The entire exercise consumed maybe twelve minutes of raw tape. We didn't need more. Why waste time?

## Spontaneous Ignition in a News Story

Our Raiders parking piece shows how spontaneous moments bring energy, and sometimes structure, to television news stories. Most won't be as obvious as that fender bender, but, by being open to the possibilities, you'll begin to notice that they present themselves more often than you might otherwise realize.

Preferably, when we cover news events, we also capture them. Stand back and look around. Like streams and rivers, story lines can have eddies and currents. Don't be afraid to let them lead you places. The pictures and sound don't have to be perfect. Viewers like to be witnesses, seeing their news fresh, as it happens.

### CRASH, BANG, "GO RAIDERS!"
**August 2001**

[SOT]
(parking attendants wave flags to direct cars)

[TRACK]
THEY'RE PLAYING FLAG FOOTBALL AT THE NETWORK
ASSOCIATES COLISEUM TONIGHT, AND THE RAIDER
NATION DOESN'T LIKE THE GAME . . .

[SOT]
Rick Borba: "Nobody's happy."

[TRACK]
FATEFUL WORDS FROM RICK BORBA AS HE
STUBBORNLY STAKED OUT A SPACE AND WAITED
FOR FRIENDS WHO HAD ALREADY "BUMPED" INTO
EACH OTHER.

[SOT]
A friend approaches Borba, shouting: "Rick, you got
a casualty. Your wife just hit a car . . ."

[TRACK]
ON AN AFTERNOON WHEN RAIDER FANS ALREADY
FELT MALIGNED BY BEING FORCED TO PARK
BETWEEN THE LINES, THIS WAS MADE-TO-THEIR-
ORDER . . . A WRECK IN THE PARKING LOT, THREE
MINUTES INTO THE NEW SEASON AND NEW RULES.
ALL PARTIES INVOLVED BLAME AN OVERZEALOUS
PARKING ASSISTANT . . .

[SOT]
Mrs. Borba: "He said, 'Pull forward.' And I go, 'I
don't want to hit that car's door,' and he said, 'Pull
forward!' I kept refusing. But he made me drive into
the door."

[SOT]
David DeLoach, damaged car's owner: "He told the
lady to pull up. She didn't want to. He insisted, and
then she ran into my door."

[SOT]
Wayne to Rick Borba: "WHO'S RESPONSIBLE?"

Borba: "The parking guy. It sure wasn't my wife."

[TRACK]
INDIRECTLY, THEY BLAME NOT THE ATTENDANT BUT
THIS MAN, MARK KAUFMAN, THE COLISEUM'S NEW
GENERAL MANAGER. HE CHANGED THE PARKING
POLICY.

[SOT]
Mark Kaufman: "Well they don't like me because I'm
doing my job. If you look at the situation right now,
it's safe."

[TRACK]
KAUFMAN RAISED RATES, RESTRIPED THE
PAVEMENT, BEGAN TELLING PEOPLE WHERE TO
PARK, AND PUT AN END TO TRADITIONAL
TAILGATING TURF. HE CALLS IT A LIABILITY.

[SOT]
Kaufman: "You had people racing across the parking
lot in vehicles, driving through others running with
lawn chairs and ice chests on foot. They were
competing for parking spaces. It was dangerous."

[SOT]
Rick Borba examines the wreck: "Look at how this
door opens across the damn parking line. There's no
room. This is ridiculous."

[TRACK]
THERE'S A POPULAR BOOK ON THE RACKS RIGHT
NOW, ABOUT DEALING WITH CHANGE.
IT'S CALLED *WHO MOVED MY CHEESE?*
IF THIS CONTINUES, OAKLAND RAIDER FANS MAY
WANT TO DO SOME READING . . .

[SOT]
Disconsolate fan sitting on a bumper with a beer in
hand: "And this isn't even the regular season, man.
It ain't gonna work!"

## Post Script

As a postscript, it's worth noting that, one hour after the fender
bender, Rick Borba, his wife, and David DeLoach had exchanged
barbecue recipes, hoisted a few beers, and become pals.

They left the rest to their insurance companies.

# 9

## Using Comparison, Contrast, and Opposites as Storytelling Devices

If you ever visit Moscow, leave plenty of time to explore its subway system, the Metro. Each station is an elaborate and individual work of art, with walls and floors made of granites and semi-precious stones. Metro stations are like hybrids of underground palaces, basilicas, and fortresses. But that's how Joseph Stalin envisioned them, as grand tributes to socialism that also doubled as bomb shelters.

The station called Revolution Square has a theme of utopian murals and bigger-than-life bronze statues. While waiting for a train, you stand next to imposing forms of the Mother, the Father, the Doctor, the Scientist, the Farmer, or other proud-looking heroes of the working class.

KGO-TV sent me to Moscow in the winter of 1992 for a series of stories about Russia's transition to a free-market economy. It was a difficult project, so I was grateful to receive help from Maxim Tkachenko, a local producer, and Sergey Gorychev, a freelance photographer. When on foreign assignment, it's always good to partner with people who know the landscape. Together, we worked a series of exhausting but exhilarating sixteen-hour days.

During that week, Maxim showed me a not-so-pretty picture of his country's economic predicament. Inflation had rendered the ruble almost worthless. Average Russians spent hours waiting for items that we would take for granted. A line for toothbrushes might extend out the door and into the street. For milk or chicken, it would wind around a corner.

After the end of our last scheduled shoot, Maxim and I hit the town for a small celebration. Details are fuzzy because we drank plenty of vodka, but I remember how we walked it off by circling Red Square in a midnight snowstorm, and that I never felt the cold. It's a wonderful memory.

On our way home we passed through the Revolution Square station for what must have been the tenth time that week, but, with all that vodka in me, inspiration struck. I saw those statues in contrast with the flesh-and-blood citizens standing around them. The real people looked exhausted and demoralized while the statues, in their noble, idealistic poses, appeared to mock them.

It inspired one last piece, using the statues and people as counterpoints:

## THE METRO
### January 1992

[TRACK]
FIFTEEN KOPECS.
IN AMERICAN MONEY, THEY'RE WORTH A LITTLE
MORE THAN ONE TENTH OF AN ABE LINCOLN
PENNY, BUT IN MOSCOW . . .

[SOT]
(coins into slot)

[TRACK]
FIFTEEN KOPECS WILL STILL BUY A TICKET TO
UTOPIA . . .

[SOT]
(people on escalator)

[TRACK]
THIS IS THE METRO . . . A SUBTERRANEAN WORLD
WITH A TRANSIENT POPULATION OF EIGHT MILLION
PEOPLE A DAY. THEY COME, THEY GO . . . AT FORTY-
FIVE SECOND INTERVALS.

[SOT]
(train arrival)

[STAND-UP]
CRITICS CALL THE METRO THE ONE PRODUCT OF
COMMUNISM THAT REALLY WORKED. THEY SAY
THAT, IF AN OUTSIDER CAME HERE AND SAW ONLY
THIS, HE MIGHT CONCLUDE THE COMMUNISTS HAD
BUILT A PERFECT WORLD.

[SOT]
(subway car door closes)

[TRACK]
STALIN ENVISIONED THE METRO AS A GRAND
MONUMENT TO SOCIALISM. EVERY STATION IS LIKE
A PALACE OR ART MUSEUM, BUT WITH DIFFERENT
THEMES—
GLASS . . .
MURALS . . .
AND IN REVOLUTION SQUARE—STATUES.
THIS IS THE MOST HAUNTING STATION OF THEM
ALL.

[SOT]
Young man in his mid-20s: "These are my
grandparents. My parents. They believed in what
they were doing. And finally they found out their
ideals were an illusion . . . nothing. This is a
station of tragedy, frankly. This is a big
tragedy."

[TRACK]
BUT HIS ANCESTORS ARE STILL HERE AND BIGGER
THAN LIFE—NOBLE FIGURES OF THE WORKING
CLASS, CAST IN BRONZE WITH STRENGTH AND
ENERGY.
THE DOCTOR . . .
THE FARMER . . .
THE ENGINEER . . .

[SOT]
First Russian male: "It's sad, really. Sad. Sad that the
people who made these people believed in what

they were doing and yet they were betrayed. They
were betrayed by themselves, by their very own
ideals. This is sad."

[TRACK]
THE STATUES NEVER MOVE. THEY NEVER CHANGE
EXPRESSION. THEY'RE FROZEN IN A WORLD OF
FAITH AND PURPOSE, BUT NOT THE WORLD
OF TODAY.
IF YOU'RE LOOKING FOR THE TRUTH IN MOSCOW,
EXAMINE ITS LIVING.

[SOT]
Old woman: "I am a pensioner. An invalid. I worked
forty-two years and now I can hardly buy bread.
The system has fallen apart."

[SOT]
Older man: "Even in childhood, these statues didn't
have a place in my world. I was in prison a long
time. I served in labor camp."

[TRACK]
THROUGHOUT HISTORY AND CULTURES, MEN HAVE
USED STATUES TO PORTRAY IDEALS AND INSPIRE
FUTURE GENERATIONS.
IT'S THE HOPE THAT LIFE WILL IMITATE ART.
BUT NOT HERE, NOT ANY LONGER.
IN RUSSIA, TIMES HAVE CHANGED.

[SOT]
(train goes away)

# 1 + 1 = 3: The Theory of Opposites

Our essay in Revolution Square used comparison, contrast, and opposites as a storytelling tool. In simpler forms, reporters use the technique almost every day. It's as basic as getting two sides of a story.

Sometimes you can build an entire piece around opposites. In
other cases you use them for reference. In September of 2000, during a heat wave in San Francisco, we used opposites both ways, one
and then the other, on consecutive days.

San Francisco had endured ninety-degree temperatures for more
than a week. Such numbers might not sound so severe to the rest of
the country, but they are to us. We call that time of year our Indian
Summer, and this one had lasted so long that we'd begun to run out
of story ideas. A guy can cover only so many ice cream factories,
blacktop pavement crews, heatstroke victims, and threats of electrical brownouts.

We'd also used up our share of luck. On the ninth day, while
shooting yet another general story about heat, I spotted a group of
young, drop-dead gorgeous people in front of a coffee shop. Despite the ninety-degree heat they wore scarves, sweaters, and
parkas.

Huh?

We learned they were fashion models doing a photo shoot for
the upcoming winter collection on, of all days, that day, the hottest
of the year. This was a contrast, made-to-order. Across the street
and all around, people were hot, sweaty, sticky, miserable, and
wearing as little as possible, but not the poor models. They wore
furs, and full-length leather coats. Worse yet, they weren't supposed
to sweat.

By including those models, we rounded out our piece. But you
can't rest on your laurels in television news. As soon as that story

aired, our executive producer at the time, Dennis Milligan, wanted to know, "What do you have for tomorrow?"

## The Hot Day: If You Steal an Idea, Take It from Yourself

I had nothing, except a crazy idea. Twenty years earlier, while working in Louisville, Kentucky, I'd done a heat wave story by using scenes from a blizzard the preceding winter. When Milligan asked about tomorrow, I remembered Louisville.

"We'll do a rain story," I said.

He didn't see the humor. "It's not raining tomorrow. It's going to be ninety-eight."

"Trust me."

Milligan did, but barely. When a reporter establishes a pattern of coming through for his bosses, they'll begin to give him some leeway, especially when those bosses don't have a better idea. Dennis didn't. Nobody did. But he trusted me.

Twenty years after the Louisville piece, San Francisco had just endured a wet El Niño winter. I went to the archives, pulling file of mud, flooding, and miserable people.

The story begins with man-on-the street interviews. Sweating people complain about the heat.

"It feels like Phoenix," says one.

"You sweat all the time," adds another.

Having established misery, we cut to a shot of me driving. I turn to the camera and ask viewers if they would want to trade summer for winter. The camera nods yes. Like a magician, I snap my fingers and, on the sound, we cut to a shot of rain pelting that very same windshield six months earlier. With this visual gimmick, we transport viewers to a wet winter, and put a different spin on the heat wave:

## INDIAN SUMMER
### September 2000

[TRACK]
WE CALL IT INDIAN SUMMER, AND, WHILE THE
NAME MAY NOT BE POLITICALLY CORRECT, HERE IT
IS, AGAIN. . . . RIGHT ON TIME.

[SOT]
Shirtless man on the street: "The Native American
people do not own this time of year. It's for all of
us . . ."

[TRACK]
A TIME TO SEEK SHADE . . . TO SAVOR OR PERHAPS
EVEN SUFFER BENEATH SWELTERING, SUNBURST
SKIES.

[SOT]
Woman in shade: "It feels like Phoenix."

[SOT]
Second woman: "You sweat all the time."

[SOT]
Third woman: "It's so hot you can't sleep."

[SOT]
(Wayne driving car)
I'M NOT A BIG FAN OF HOT DAYS LIKE THIS, EITHER.
ARE YOU?
(camera shakes back and forth: "NO.")
EVER THINK WISTFULLY OF WINTER?
WISH YOU COULD GO BACK?

(camera nods: "YES")
SURE?
(camera nods: "YES")
OK . . .
(Wayne snaps fingers)

[SOT]
(cut to shot from winter, looking out the front of a windshield in a driving rain storm)

[TRACK]
WHOA! WHAT HAPPENED?

[SOT]
Man in file tape during rain storm: "It was quite an adrenaline rush."

[TRACK]
ACTUALLY, IT'S A DELUGE. WELCOME BACK TO THE LAND OF LA NIÑA, THE HELL OF EL NIÑO—THE WETTER SIDE OF WINTER. OR HAD YOU FORGOTTEN?

[SOT]
(file of woman downtown woman in rain)
Wayne to woman: "YOUR HAIR IS REACTING REALLY WELL TO THIS."

Woman: "You mean my frizz?"

[TRACK]
WE MEAN, YOU ASKED FOR IT. YOU'VE TRADED HEAT WAVES ON PAVEMENT FOR THE AQUATIC

VARIETY, AND GREEN GRASS FOR MOUNTAINS OF
MUD.
YOU'RE BACK IN THE AIRPORT NOW, THE VICTIM OF
ANOTHER WEATHER DELAY.

[SOT]
Man in airport during weather delay: "The travel
agent should have warned us."

[TRACK]
NO, YOU SHOULD HAVE REMEMBERED HOW, LAST
WINTER, WE SUFFERED THROUGH MORE THAN ONE
HUNDRED CONSECUTIVE DAYS OF RAIN.

[SOT]
File of construction worker in rain: "Today I need my
weather boots. My back is soaked."

[TRACK]
THE DELUGE CONTINUED INTO MARCH, APRIL, MAY.
BY THEN, WE CONSIDERED BUILDING ARKS.

[SOT]
Frizzy-haired woman: "I'm sick of this. It's like the
seven plagues. It's Biblical . . ."

[TRACK]
AND YOU ASKED FOR IT.

[SOT]
(Wayne, on camera, snaps fingers)
BUT ENOUGH ALREADY. TWO MONTHS FROM NOW,
IT WILL BE COLD AND WET AND WINDY AND WE'LL

> BE WISHING FOR BEAUTIFUL WEATHER LIKE THIS, SO
> LET'S ENJOY IT WHILE WE HAVE IT . . . EVERY
> SINGLE SWEATY SECOND.

Opposites work in stories because they illuminate the true natures of people, places, things, and events. To appreciate black, you need to know white. It's the same with good and evil, communism and autocracy, hot and cold, or any other subject you might deem appropriate.

Comparison and contrast is just another of those reporter tricks, but keep it in mind for a rainy day—or maybe a hot one.

# 10

---

## Stand-Ups

---

Every year, a new group of interns and production assistants comes to work in our news department. Predictably, some of them will say they want to report, and then request the staff's help in preparing so-called résumé tapes. Long before these interns ask about what makes a story, or how to conduct interviews, or write, or edit, most will mention the need to "shoot a few stand-ups," as if they imagine that's the foremost job qualification. In watching them, one gets a feeling they want to work *in* television for the thrill of getting *on* television.

Someone needs to tell these wannabes they have it backwards.

I've always thought being on television should be a byproduct of reporting, not the ultimate goal. The rest of the job comes first. Television news isn't about the presenters.

## Stand-Up Basics

Reporters do stand-ups for a number of reasons:

1. Stand-ups help reporters describe what they can't otherwise show, including the past, the future, or concepts.
2. Stand-ups provide an extra production element. When a reporter has a visually challenging story, every new scene helps keep a piece moving.
3. Stand-ups allow reporters to turn story lines in different directions.
4. Stand-ups help reporters confide, or make an aside, or take a time out from the main body of a piece.

It's only natural for young reporters to struggle when learning to speak to the camera. They ask similar questions.

"How do I act?"

"What should I do?"

"What do I say?"

"When do I say it?"

Those are normal concerns. Though the years, I've developed a number of techniques and guidelines for dealing with them. Maybe they'll also help you:

## When Not to Do a Stand-Up

Although it is difficult to learn how and when to use a stand-up, it's equally important to learn when not to do one. We reporters may worship the sights and sounds of ourselves on television, but we often make the mistake of forgetting that we, too, are talking heads—and, often, obtrusive ones. In the wrong place or with the wrong tone, a stand-up can hurt a piece. Reporters make this mistake at every professional level, including the networks.

A few years ago, I sat on an Emmy Award panel and judged features from a top-three market. One entry followed a high-school girl who played on the varsity football team, won the title of homecoming queen, and then kicked a winning field goal, all in the same night. Panel members loved this piece until the last few seconds. Then, instead of finishing with a classic shot of the girl walking off the field, the reporter did a stand-up close.

What could he have been thinking? It was a classic example of how stand-ups ruin stories more often than they help them.

## Use a Wireless Lapel Microphone

Unless you're working in a loud environment and need the superior sound qualities of a stick microphone, wear a lapel microphone instead. It frees your hands, allowing you to gesture, or lean on or touch something. You'll feel more comfortable and communicate more effectively.

## Find Friendly Light

Nobody looks good in direct sunlight. It casts dark, harsh shadows. Sunlight makes you scrunch your face. As an alternative, find open shade or a location where your photographer can put a flattering light or two on you.

If, for reasons beyond control, you cannot avoid the sun, minimize your time on camera. Find a reason to keep the shot wide. One method might be to establish a presence at the scene, say a few words, point to something, and have the camera follow.

# Do Stand-Up Bridges

You don't see many stand-up opens these days, but, as in the case of that reporter who covered the homecoming queen, some of us do too many stand-up closes, often out of habit. Stand-up closes tend to detract from central characters or narrative story lines, unless they never existed.

Generally, it's good practice to do a stand-up bridge in the first half of a story. Why? The later you appear in a piece, the greater your risk of intruding, although this isn't a hard-and-fast rule. If I do a bridge in the second half of a story, it's usually to reveal a twist.

# Contemplate Fit and Flow

Anticipate how a stand-up will suit the rest of the piece. Does it fit into the pacing, or distract from it? Should you add movement, or simply stand and talk?

Weigh the story's content, mood, and pacing. You want to be natural when on camera, but don't try too hard. Don't sling a jacket over your shoulder to affect a look. Avoid being touchy-feely just for the sake of it. If your news director asks for you to walk and point, do so for the benefit of your viewers. If you kneel down and pick up dry leaves that might be clogging a storm drain, finish the move by showing them to the camera, up close.

In order to come across as a normal person, act like one. If you're in a garage, for example, don't begin your stand-up by sliding out from a car unless you're actually working on it. In three words, be a reporter. Don't pretend to be anything else.

## Note Your Composition in the Frame

Note where your interview subjects appear in the picture. Are they facing screen right or screen left? Are they big or small? If you'll be leading into or following an interviewee's sound bite with a stand-up, try to juxtapose your head or body into a different part of the frame, and at a different size. Good composition makes for cleaner edits.

## Why Are You Walking and Talking?

Before he died too young, former NBC News correspondent Bob Elliott returned to Portland, Maine, where he worked several years as a feature reporter and social commentator. Bob liked to poke fun at everyday life. In his stories, he regularly used himself and a re-volving cast of characters, including his friends, his wife, and his soft-spoken father. Viewers particularly loved the senior Elliott. But then Dad decided he'd spent enough winters in Maine, and an-nounced he was moving to southern Florida.

Before the old man left town, Bob reprised his father's televi-sion "career." In that piece, Mr. Elliott hints how he plans to land a better gig in a bigger market, Miami. Bob tells his dad he'll need to make a résumé tape, and shows him how to do it, spoofing the industry.

The piece has a wonderful scene in which Bob tries to teach his dad how to do a stand-up: "Walk, Dad. Just walk and talk."

"Why do reporters walk when they talk?" his father asks.

"I don't know. They just do. They do it too much. Now walk, anyway. But start talking first."

Bob was correct. People *do* walk and talk too much in stand-ups, and it shows. Why are they walking? Where are they going?

But it looks even worse when reporters begin walking after they start talking.

If you must have movement, try this alternative. Stand in one spot. Have the camera push in to you. This is more dignified than walking. As the shot tightens, it adds importance to whatever you're saying.

And, while we're discussing zooms, I would caution you against doing a stand-up in which the camera pulls back. Even when a shot widens to reveal something, it can kill a story's momentum. Why should viewers pay attention to a visually shrinking reporter? It's the equivalent of trying to listen to someone when he's walking away.

## Use the Medium

Not every stand-up must originate in the field. When warranted, you might work with an electronic chroma-key, the same technology we use to insert maps behind weather forecasters.

Let's say you need to explain the moving parts of an airliner's tail section. Obviously, you can't go to the airport, climb a ladder, and do the stand-up there, but you can use the chroma-key to insert a close-up picture behind you as you do a walk-around in the studio. Point to the parts of that tail as a weather forecaster would point to a storm front.

### Split the Screen and Make a List

If you're working a fact-heavy, nonvisual story, split the screen and make a list. Have the photographer frame you in the right-hand side of his screen, leaving room for postproduction graphics to appear on the left. As you run down the list on camera, have each item appear as a bullet point, to which you nod or refer.

Why should you be on the right and the words on the left? Simple. That's how people read—from the left.

## You Need Not Speak Directly to the Viewer

Try a stand-up in which you never speak directly to the camera, but still include the viewers.

Photographer Scott Arthur tried this technique when we visited a secret room atop San Francisco's Transamerica Pyramid. It's a tiny glass lookout barely big enough for two people and one very bright beacon. To get there, a person must climb more than two hundred steps, and then a precarious-looking ladder.

We began our segment in the express elevator. As it beeped upward through the floors, viewers saw chief building engineer Mike Bellafronte and me staring straight ahead:

> [TRACK]
> BY ELEVATOR STANDARDS, THIS PUSHES THE
> ENVELOPE FOR LONG HAULS. HOW ELSE WOULD
> YOU EXPLAIN TWO MEN OBSERVING PROTOCOL BY
> MINDING THEIR OWN BUSINESS, IN THEIR OWN
> SPACE, AS TIME DRAGS BY IN A SMALL, UPWARDLY
> MOBILE BOX?
>
> [WAYNE ON CAMERA]
> Wayne turns to Bellafronte and, with the camera
> looking over Bellafronte's shoulder toward him, asks:
> "WHY DON'T PEOPLE SPEAK TO EACH OTHER IN
> ELEVATORS?"
>
> Mike: "It's not proper elevator etiquette."

Although I addressed my query to the engineer, it also included the viewers, who might as well have been riding with us. And who, at one time or another, hasn't asked that question of himself?

# A One-Word Stand-Up

Several years ago, KGO-TV photographer Cathy Cavey and I traveled to Carvers, Nevada, a tiny cluster of businesses in the desert. When their owner put them up for sale, he essentially put the entire town up for sale, as well.

Our route took us along Highway 50, which Nevadans describe as "the loneliest highway in America." After about a hundred miles, Cathy asked, "When do we get there?"

"Hours," I replied, in a bored and sarcastic tone, and that gave us an idea. We would do a stand-up consisting of one word. Here's how it worked, surrounded by the narration leading in and out:

> [TRACK]
> TO GET TO CARVERS, WE RENTED A CAR AND THEN
> DROVE, AND DROVE, AND DROVE, FOR. . . .
>
> [WAYNE ON CAMERA]
> Wayne turns from the steering wheel and says:
> "HOURS . . . ."
>
> [TRACK]
> . . . ABOUT FOUR HOURS AND TWO HUNDRED FIFTY
> MILES SOUTHEAST OF RENO.
> OUT THROUGH THE MOONSCAPE . . .
> OUT PAST THE SAND DUNES . . .
> OUT WHERE OLD BEER BOTTLES CRACK IN THE
> SUN . . .
> OUT TO WHERE WINDMILLS HAVE BULLET HOLES . . .
> AND STOP SIGNS MUST WAVE FOR YOUR
> ATTENTION . . .

With one short word, we described a very long trip.

# Write into and Out of Your Stand-Up As You Would Any Other Piece of Sound

Look back once again at that that one-word stand-up. Notice how the narration leads into my one word on camera, and then resumes, as in one thought. Technically, a stand-up is no different than any other sound bite. Transitions shouldn't call attention to themselves.

## Stay in the Moment

A few years ago, the desk sent photographer Randy Davis and me to cover Tiger Woods as he played in his first AT&T golf tournament. Woods had just turned professional and, because he had Kevin Costner for his partner, the crowd swelled, making it almost impossible to get a good shot of either man.

We decided our best option would be to turn to turn that negative into a positive. Just before the stand-up, I wrote to pictures of the difficult viewing conditions:

> [TRACK]
> . . . TO BE MORE PRECISE, YOU DON'T SEE THEIR
> SHOTS AS MUCH AS LISTEN FOR THEM. THAT LITTLE
> DOT DOWN THERE IS THE YOUNG TIGER AS HE
> MISSES A PUTT . . .
>
> [SOT]
> The crowd loudly sighs: "Augh."
>
> [TRACK]
> . . . AND NOW, KEVIN COSTNER TEES OFF. HE MAY

DANCE WITH WOLVES, BUT HE ALSO SLICES INTO
THE WOODS . . .

[SOT]
Costner hits a horrendous shot. The crowd moans:
"Oooooh."

[TRACK]
. . . CLEARLY, ONE OF LIFE'S GREAT TRAGEDIES . . .

Here we cut to my stand-up. We intended to do a walk through the
gallery, but the crowd didn't cooperate. I couldn't finish a sentence
without someone stepping in front of the camera, so, again, we
used that to our advantage. In a long-lens shot surrounded by people, I said:

[STAND-UP]
IT'S HARD TO BELIEVE, BUT WE SPENT ABOUT AN
HOUR TRYING TO GET JUST ONE GOOD SHOT OF
THOSE GUYS AND . . .

Now a golf cart stopped and blocked Randy's shot. I was flustered,
but I stayed in the moment and ad-libbed:

[STAND-UP CONTINUES]
. . . UGH . . . AND . . . OH WELL. MAYBE WE
SHOULD GIVE UP AND TRY TO GET PICTURES OF
SOMEONE ELSE.

We never planned for that golf cart to stop between us, but it
helped show the difficulties of getting from place to place. Randy
and I had worked together long enough that he knew to keep the
camera rolling. That ad-lib worked better than any stand-up we
might have scripted.

# Adapt to Your Environment: The 360-Degree Stand-Up

As you do more stand-ups, you'll begin to recognize the visual and editorial possibilities, or lack of them, in every story and location.

Again with Cathy Cavey behind the lens, we covered the aftermath of a warehouse fire. This one was unusual because, before the place burned, its tenant, a guy named Stephen, had collected dozens of old pianos, and mounted them from floor to ceiling. Moreover, he placed those pianos in chronological, clockwise order, from oldest to newest, as an artistic statement. It made an eerily unusual sight.

As I stood in one spot and spoke, Cathy made a clockwise, 360-degree pan around the room. Here are the words:

> [STAND-UP]
> YOU CAN'T TELL FROM THE CHARRED REMNANTS,
> BUT THOSE PIANOS ARE STACKED IN
> CHRONOLOGICAL ORDER. THAT'S 1865 OVER THERE,
> THE END OF THE CIVIL WAR. AND IF YOU MOVE
> CLOCKWISE AROUND THE ROOM, YOU CAN TRACE
> MORE HISTORY AS YOU WOULD WITH THE RINGS OF
> A TREE, OR NUMBERS ON A CLOCK FACE. NOW
> WE'RE PASSING THE TURN OF THE CENTURY.
> THERE'S WORLD WAR I, AND BEHIND ME HERE—
> 1930. IT'S THE NEWEST PIANO STEVEN KEPT. HE
> SAYS THAT'S WHEN THEY STOPPED MAKING GOOD
> ONES . . .

## James Dean

The James Dean Memorial near Cholame, along California's central coast, is a peculiar place. It sits in front of a small post office just below Polonio Pass on Route 46, not far from where the movie star died in his 1955 Porsche Spyder. All day, every day, tourists drive miles out of their way to stop at the spot and take pictures. Most of them can't even explain why. It's just something to do.

Lilly Grant, who ran that post office, insisted she isn't a James Dean fan, but, because of the many questions she has fielded from curious people, she probably knows more about his death than anyone else on Earth. "I can't see what his fans saw in him," Lilly confided.

What Lilly liked best about James Dean was telling stories about him. For the most exuberant visitors, she would go so far as to produce police photographs of the accident scene. "Some of these people ask about James Dean's last coke bottle," said Lilly, with a wry laugh.

"What coke bottle?"

"He's supposed to have stopped for a coke a few minutes before he died," she explained. "They think the bottle flew from the car, and wonder if anybody found it."

Around sunset, photographer Clyde Powell and I went to do a stand-up at the accident site. We tried a few takes, describing what happened there so many years before. As the sun dropped lower, I began to squint, and realized that, when James Dean came down the same road in similar conditions, he probably squinted, too.

I changed a few words and, with Clyde, choreographed a move. From my starting point, I walked past Clyde, who moved backward to a second position, where the camera "squints" into the sun to see me. Then we reversed that move to finish where we started.

[STAND-UP]
(position 1: looking up road)
BY NOW THE STORY OF WHAT HAPPENED HERE HAS
BECOME PART OF THE LEGEND. JAMES DEAN CAME

DOWN THIS HILL DOING PERHAPS EIGHTY MILES AN
HOUR IN HIS SMALL PORSCHE CONVERTIBLE. HE
PASSED ONE CAR AND THEN A SECOND CAR
BLOCKED HIM IN.

(position 2: camera squints into sunset)
AT THAT MOMENT, HE WAS BLINDED BY THE SUN
SETTING BEYOND THOSE COASTAL HILLS . . .

(position 3: looking up road again)
BY THE TIME HE COULD SEE AGAIN, IT WAS TOO
LATE TO AVOID A THIRD CAR MAKING A LEFT TURN
IN THE INTERSECTION AHEAD.

Clyde and I didn't recognize it at the time, but that was a darn near perfect stand-up.

We described something we couldn't show—an automobile accident.

We gave the details of what happened.

We used movement.

Better still, we put viewers into James Dean's place by showing them what he saw in his last conscious seconds. Stand-ups don't get much better than that.

# 11

## Face Time: Going Live

Regular viewers don't know this, but some of the most entertaining television news never makes air. Oh, it's available, all right, but, unless you're one of the gang in transmission or have a special satellite receiver at home, you'll miss the show.

It isn't a program. It hasn't an official name, channel, or time slot. It stars any reporter with access to a camera, a dish, and a satellite window. If you're curious about a reporter's nature, observe him in the moments just before he takes his cue from an anchor. How does he handle the pressure? Is he in a good mood, or sniping at the crew? It's always worth a chuckle to watch some snarling grouse who, seconds before going live, miraculously changes demeanor from black cloud to teevee perky.

For a time, I collected some of these performances. To that end,

our transmission people monitored satellite feeds and recorded reporters standing in adverse conditions—blizzards, hurricanes,
swamps populated by bloodthirsty mosquitoes. That's what we do,
right? It's part of the unwritten job description. At the first hint of
bad weather, management sends us into the elements with orders
to stand there, absorbing nature's abuse like experimental test
strips. "Thanks," the anchors inevitably say. "You're a trouper."

More than once, while doubling as a human rain gauge, I've been
tempted to cut loose and tell viewers the truth. "Yes, this is how
ridiculous you, too, could look if you chose television news reporting for a career."

Actually, I have said those words, but never on air, merely when
waiting, and only to a satellite thousand of miles above, along with
anyone watching below. More than once I have dared phantom
viewers to guess my location. "Here's my pager number. Go ahead
and dial—it's on vibrate. Reach out and tickle me. If you name the
place and story, we'll send you a promotional Circle 7 lapel pin."

One guy actually did call once from somewhere in Connecticut.
He only missed by three time zones and a sunset that, for us, hadn't
happened yet. Then again, he'd been drinking.

We sent him a promotional Circle 7 lapel pin, anyway.

Frankly, unless a reporter has a deep-seated craving for face time,
doing a live shot usually complicates an assignment. Live shots
shorten deadlines and frazzle reporters, who must race from the
site of a story, back to the station for editing, and then return to the
location. Either that, or they remain at the scene, spending the day
in a small truck that gets hot in summer and cold in winter. In
terms of square footage, Apollo astronauts had more room.

# Live Shots Are Here to Stay

If you get the impression that live shots are not my favorite part of the job, you're correct. I'm not alone in thinking that television news has abused the technology, and turned live shots into a crutch. Where reporters used to craft stories with pictures and sound, now they're just as likely to stand and talk. Instead of showing the news, many stations settle for reporters pointing at the news, and telling it.

But live shots come with the territory. They are to newscasts what George Washington is to the dollar bill. Producers and other managers defend them with the same ferocity as mothers protecting their young. They believe live shots add production value or immediacy to a newscast. Often, they do. And, just as often, they don't.

When you're in the field, expect that some live-shot assignments won't make sense. 'Tis not your job to reason. It won't help to argue. For the sake of your career, just smile and do the job. Your producers may have unseen pressures.

"Tell me the truth," I once asked our noon producer, Leetha Yee. "Why do you need this live shot so badly?"

"I need you to go live because we're short of writers," she confessed. "Just stand there and tell us what you know. I don't have enough people to work the copy or edit tape. They called in sick."

At least she was honest. I have to respect that.

# The Positives

But, in fairness, live shots do have a place and purpose. Used properly, they allow reporters to do their jobs faster and more effectively.

If news has just broken or continues developing, reporters can use live shots to give viewers the latest information. If an assignment is lean in terms of visuals or people, or if a reporter couldn't physically cover every aspect of a story, or if he arrived late, the live shot lets him fill in the blanks. He can tell viewers what he knows, or with whom he just spoke, and give other pertinent details.

Having weighed the positives and negatives, I offer some guidelines to help you do better live shots.

# Speak Naturally, Even Casually

Don't worry if you get nervous before going live. It's natural. Go easy on yourself. Relax. In live shots, you're just talking, the same as anywhere else.

Reporters get into live-shot trouble when they try to speak as precisely as they write. Don't bother to try memorizing a live shot. Learn to talk on the fly as you would to a friend, a producer, or the assignment desk. Think of it this way: Do you stumble in ordinary conversation? Probably no more than when you walk down a street. The same principle applies in live shots. Speak normally and keep it simple.

## Use Key Words for Notes, Not Sentences

You might have an easier time learning to talk a live shot if you write down two or three key words. Use them as a word trail and follow them, the same as you would steps along a path.

I remember doing a live shot after a fatal collision between two fire-fighting planes. We stood outside the air base. On my notepad, I wrote "flowers" for my first key word, referencing the gate in front of the base:

> FLOWERS AND NOTES PINNED TO THE GATE TELL A
> STORY OF SADNESS AND LOSS.

For the second word I wrote "privacy," because the people inside the base asked us to keep a respectful distance:

> THIS IS A CLOSE GROUP OF PEOPLE. THEY WORK
> TOGETHER AND PLAY TOGETHER AND, TONIGHT,
> THEY'RE ASKING FOR PRIVACY AS THEY GRIEVE
> TOGETHER . . .

I ad-libbed those words. For most live shots, I usually write only the roll cue in full, using big letters, surrounded with brackets so they're easy to see:

> FIGHTING FIRES WITH AIRPLANES HAS ALWAYS BEEN
> RISKY.
> CREWS KNOW IT.
> THEY ACCEPT IT.
> TONIGHT THEY'RE DEALING WITH IT . . .

If I ever get lost or tongue-tied while doing a live shot (and this does happen), it's reassuring to know I can refer to my notes and use that one complete line to bail into the package or sound bite.

## Beware of Typical Live Clichés and Crutches

> AS YOU CAN SEE BEHIND ME . . .
> EVEN AS WE SPEAK . . .
> LET'S TAKE A LIVE LOOK . . .
> WE WANT TO TELL YOU . . .
> OF COURSE . . .
> WE CAN REPORT . . .

The industry is full of such phrases. They're a waste of breath.

One of the worst is the word *Now.* Watch certain reporters, and count the number of sentences beginning with, *"Now . . ."* The word is an affectation of immediacy, usually where none exists.

## Reference Your Location

Even if you're standing in the dark for one of those notorious black-hole live shots with nothing visible in the background, give viewers a sense of where you are and what happened there. Set a scene. Paint a picture with words:

> THE MEETING ENDED OFFICIALLY AT NINE O'CLOCK,
> BUT, LONG AFTER THE DOORS CLOSED, IT
> CONTINUED IN THIS PARKING LOT.

# Go Mobile

When doing live shots in locations with visual possibilities, consider asking the photographer to hand-hold the camera. Use it to take the viewer somewhere. Reporters have done excellent live shots in which they stood outside a door, opened it a crack, and let the camera peek inside. That's good stuff. It's voyeuristic and has the look of being live. The lens becomes a window and the reporter, a guide.

## Change the Background Between Your Introduction and Tag

When possible and appropriate, change the background between your introduction to a package and its tag. While the story runs, turn 180 degrees, or move somewhere else, or at least change the background to give the viewers a different look.

Photographer Doug Lauglin and I used the technique when a B-24 bomber flew into town as part of an air show exhibit. We shot a story, cut it in the field, and, later, wrapped a live shot around it. For the introduction, we stood outside the plane. Then, as the piece played, we hurried to a second location inside the cockpit where Doug had rigged a small video camera. He plugged it in and we closed the live report by crawling through the old bomber, taking viewers along what would have been a crew's escape route from the cockpit to the hatch, two decks below. It wasn't so much a live-shot tag as a short journey.

## Hide Your Earpiece

When doing live shots, every reporter uses an earpiece through which he hears the anchors, the producer, the director, and cues. We call it an *Interruptible Feedback Device,* or *IFB.*

The best of these are custom-molded to your ear and become almost invisible, but, even then, wear the IFB on the side you'll least show the camera. This is one of those finesse touches that makes a good impression on résumé tapes.

## Match Your Voice Between the Introduction and Track

Early in their careers, reporters tend to read narrative tracks in a different tone of voice, or at a different energy level, than when they speak live. News directors look for this on résumé tapes, and regard it as a sign of inexperience. Seasoned reporters usually sound the same, whether speaking or reading.

Here are three ways to sound more consistent:

1. Use the same microphone in your live shot as you did for your narrative track. No two microphones sound exactly alike.
2. As you read your track, talk it. Look at the script, but imagine being in front of a teleprompter, speaking to a camera.
3. Use a short section of natural sound at the top of the story before that track begins. With as little as a two-second break, you can mask any vocal or technical inconsistencies.

# Add a Production Element

Even if you're only doing a quick live hit with a voiceover into a sound bite, add a production element.

Only two days before this writing, a sewer blew up in downtown San Francisco. No one knew the cause, but the blast shattered windows and tossed two heavy manhole covers twenty feet into the air. The producer asked for a live shot with a voiceover, followed by one or two sound bites, my choice. That's where I added the wrinkle. Rather than the conventional method of placing both sound bites at the end of a live voiceover, I used one of them, a witness who had seen the explosions, at the beginning.

Live on camera, I gave the director a roll cue and let that first sound bite run. Then, on the same piece of tape, we butted trailing video for use in a live voiceover. This enabled me to begin reading from the end of the sound bite, without waiting for a cue and risking an awkward delay. As that voiceover ended, the director knew to roll a second tape with the other sound bite. While it played, I took a few steps to my left to change the background, and then tagged the segment live on camera.

Sound complicated? It wasn't—just fast and efficient. From two pieces of tape we gave the live shot three components: a sound bite, a voiceover, and another sound bite. When you count the live ledes and tags with slightly different backgrounds, we did a 1:15 segment utilizing five different looks.

# Structure the Package

As with any other story, a live-shot insert should be able to stand alone, with a beginning, middle, and ending. Without such structure, we regress to the standards of thirty or forty years ago, when reporters did packages with stand-up opens and closes. Sometimes, adding structure means only two extra lines, one for the beginning and another to conclude.

Here's the open photographer Randy Davis and I used when covering a convicted murderer's clemency hearing. The piece begins with strained faces of people in an auditorium:

> [TRACK]
> THESE ARE THE FACES OF VICTIMS. BETWEEN THEM
> THEY SHARE FOUR MURDERS, TWELVE RAPES, AND
> SEVENTEEN YEARS OF WAITING FOR DARRYL RICH
> TO DIE.
>
> [SOT]
> Friend of a victim: "I would support clemency if he
> were a human being, but this isn't a man. He's a
> monster."

It's a small touch, but small touches add up when you're building a professional reputation. By giving your live-shot insert a distinct beginning, middle, and ending, subsequent broadcasts can take that package and use it again without additional editing. Later, if a network feed picks it up, the extra effort may also put some coin in your pocket.

# Keep a Copy of the Package Script in Your Hand

CBS News correspondent John Blackstone learned this lesson the hard way, after twenty-one years at the network. He was covering a major trial in San Francisco, and would use a live shot to introduce a package following a late-in-the-day verdict. As Blackstone set up live on the bureau roof, he heard the producer in New York tell him, "Stand by. We're having a technical difficulty with your feed."

Six or seven minutes passed. John waited, and finally heard the introduction from Dan Rather. Simultaneously, that same producer broke in on his IFB: "John, we never did get a clean version of the package. Just talk to Dan. You have a minute and a half."

Poor Blackstone. "That's not what I expected," he said. "I'd prepared two sentences as a lead-in." Now he would have to more or less recite the script, but he hadn't brought the copy with him.

Despite his quickened heartbeat and elevated blood pressure, Blackstone did a flawless talk-back, "But it certainly would have been easier if I'd had that script in my hand for reference."

He's kept one with him for every live shot since.

## Speak with Your Anchor in Advance

Live shots should transition smoothly from the studio to the field, and back again. Whenever possible, plan these segues in advance. Help your anchors by suggesting what they might say in their introductions to you. Recommend questions they might ask when you finish. By being smart, you'll look smart.

When you're live, it is not a good time for surprises.

### Protect Yourself—Don't Tell the Anchors Everything

While it's good for a reporter and an anchor to each know what the other is doing, Don Knapp, who spent twelve years as a correspondent for CNN, warns about giving anchors too much information in advance. "The network would fly me in to a fire or whatever, get me on the ground next to the truck, and expect me to go live immediately," he says. "That was always their first priority."

As a good soldier, Don would call his producers in Atlanta and tell what he knew, even if it wasn't much. "I might say there was a fire, that people had been hurt, that we didn't know the extent of the damage yet, and that we were waiting for authorities to update the situation."

Inevitably, when leading into Knapp's live shot, the anchor would repeat all of those facts, leaving Don with nothing to add. "Protect yourself," says Knapp. "Save a detail or two—something you can work with."

## Never Directly Correct Your Anchor

In my first week at KRON-TV in San Francisco, an electrical transmission box blew up downtown, spreading carcinogenic PCBs across two city blocks. Authorities closed the area for several days.

When pitching to my live shot one night, the anchor referred repeatedly to "PCPs," which had nothing to do with smoking electrical boxes, but everything to do with smoking marijuana. I made the mistake of correcting her while on the air, and did it smugly, at that. A more seasoned reporter would have handled her mistake indirectly, by mentioning the letters PCB as often as possible.

Back at the station later that night, the anchor lay in wait with claws extended. I took maybe two steps through the door before she loudly and publicly ripped into me. "Don't you ever *dare* correct me on the air again, young man." She actually waved a flawlessly manicured red fingernail in front of my nose.

Beware the wrath of an embarrassed anchor. It leads to an even more embarrassed reporter.

After the anchor went home, our broadcast's producer, Peter Spear, took me aside and broke the tension with some hilarious but sage advice. "Welcome to big-market television, kid. Remember this lesson. Anchors ain't normal people. They like to believe they're normal people. They try to act like normal people. But they have this red-light fever affliction. When they stare at tally lights long enough, their brains scramble. Now here's the key to survival. Whatever you do and wherever you go in the rest of your career, never let on to an anchorperson that you know this secret. Indulge them. Make them feel wonderful, gifted, brilliant, and, most important, normal. But remember. Normal, they ain't."

To be fair, I have heard of and actually met some anchors who don't fit Peter's generalization. If you are an anchor and reading this, it will be only natural for you to assume you are one of them.

## Personal Horror Story

Like every other skill in this business, learning to go live takes diligence, hard work, and practice. Any honest reporter can tell his own personal live-shot horror story, and maybe two or three. Hence the adage that it's always good to make your biggest mistakes early, in markets you can leave.

My worst live shot was also my first. It happened at WLKY-TV in Louisville, Kentucky, where news director Brian Norcross, who later became a weather forecaster in Miami, gave me my first job. He hired me as a photographer, but promised occasional reporting opportunities.

Less than two weeks later, I got my first big "break." A freight train derailed in western Louisville. Actually, "derail" might be too strong a word. One wheel of one empty car of a four-car train slipped off the track. Norcross didn't have anyone else available, so he sent me. When the photographer and I got to the scene, we found a few railroad police and several mischievous teenagers.

The newscast would sign off in a few minutes. Our producer

wanted a live report. The photographer established a signal in close to record time. Actually, he got it up too fast. He put a microphone in my hand, crammed an IFB into my head and, before I knew anything pertinent, the control room told us to stand by. The first rule of live shots is to be prepared when you go on the air, and I was about to learn it.

I was already stressed, and the giggling teenagers made it worse. "We're going to be live in a minute, so please wait behind the camera and don't wave or anything, okay?" Like little angels, they smiled. But these kids weren't angels. As soon as anchor Ken Rowland pitched to our live shot, they leaped in front of the camera, waving and howling and jumping. In an effort to get the kids off camera, the photographer panned left. The kids followed.

He zoomed in tight. They pressed closer to me. He jerked left, then right, then up, then down, trying to fake them out. It didn't work. They moved just as fast.

The situation was out of control and hopeless. Plain and simple, I panicked. With the kids screaming and the camera moving, who could think? Mr. Rowland, a Louisville news institution, then asked a pertinent question. "Wayne, you didn't tell us, but where, exactly, is that derailment?"

I should have said, "You're watching it, Ken." After rushing to the scene, and having lived in town barely two weeks, I honestly did not know.

Those are the gory details of how my first live shot inadvertently became my first humorous show-closer.

If only it had been funny at the time.

# 12

## We Interrupt
## This Serious Book . . .

Time now for some black humor. If you've read this far, you deserve a literary recess.

This is the most twisted goof I ever witnessed in a newsroom. It happened in 1975, about two weeks after KABC-TV in Los Angeles took delivery of its first microwave truck, and it explains the later use of supplemental cover video, or "b-roll," during live shots. In those early days, live shots were a novelty. Reporters would stand at a scene, describing something or interviewing someone while, at the bottom of the screen, the station inserted large letters: "Live." In theory, this made a report more exciting, but viewers and news managers soon realized that live talking heads in the field weren't any more fascinating than live talking heads behind a desk.

For that reason, KABC-TV news director Bill Fyffe wrote a memo suggesting that, during extended live interviews, photographers should pan the scene to give viewers a look around.

Fyffe was a formidable boss. The man had a deep, fearsome, booming voice like that of a drill sergeant. Whenever he issued an order, staff members practically jumped to carry it out. He rarely closed his office door, but above it he hung a traffic light. If it showed green, you could enter without risk. If yellow, best to make the visit quick. And, if that light glowed red, you didn't want to imagine the consequences.

As fair warning, Fyffe also hung a plaque on his office wall. It bore the following words, a twist on the Twenty-third Psalm, "Yea, though I walk through the Valley of the Shadow of Death I shall fear no evil because I am the meanest son of a bitch in the valley."

But, actually, there was someone meaner. We knew him only by reputation, as the Trash Bag Murderer. At the time, he'd been killing transients, dismembering them, stuffing their pieces into plastic garbage bags, and leaving them along streets and highways between Los Angeles and the Mexican border.

Late one sweltering afternoon, the killer struck again. Our assignment desk sent reporter Steve Lentz, along with a photographer who shall, in deference to his good name and the rest of his career, remain unidentified. We'll call him Wally.

The crew lit up a live signal and the newscast took them immediately. Lentz stood about twenty yards in front of the bag, and questioned a Los Angeles police detective. Their interview went something like this:

LENTZ: "How long has the body been here?"

DETECTIVE: "The, uh, subject was discovered this afternoon at approximately 1637 hours . . ."

LENTZ: "Do you have any idea who the victim might be?"

DETECTIVE: "The, uh, deceased is not carrying any obvious identification."

LENTZ: "Any motive behind these killings?"

DETECTIVE: "Well, uh, no. But a motive might lead us to the perpetrator . . ."

Live or not, this interview could have a murderous effect on the ratings. The detective was really boring. "There, uh, have been several incidents of this nature in recent weeks."

About then, Wally remembered Bill Fyffe's memo, and he began a slow pan to the left. In a corner of his picture, viewers could see a black plastic bag baking in the summer sun. The cop kept rambling. "The, uh, heinous nature of the crime suggests . . ."

Having finished the pan, Wally followed his photographic instincts and hit the zoom button. At home, viewers saw their televisions fill with his image of the large, lumpy bag. It bulged from the middle and slumped from the curb.

Back in his office, Bill Fyffe blew up and stormed into the newsroom. "Dammit, Wally! Get off the bag!" he bellowed.

But it was too late. As if on cue that hot, overstuffed bag split open, revealing a second, leaking bag inside. Through its opaque plastic, viewers saw the outlines of a hand and other body parts.

Not so appropriately, a graphic at the bottom of the screen read, "Live."

How bad was it? Horrible. Grotesque. Unfathomable. Especially at the dinner hour.

"Dammit! Get off the bag!"

As if he heard Fyffe by the force of psychic energy alone, Wally panned again, tracking the gooey trail of congealing blood from the sidewalk to the curb, then to the gutter and eventually into a storm drain.

Fyffe was spewing by then. My desk sat directly outside his door, and I had an up-close look. The man was beside himself. I retreated to the microwave transmission room where, with the live shot mercifully ended, technicians rolled tape of Lentz asking a few more questions for the late news.

Even then, the detective never changed his dreary tone. Lentz, who has always been a joker, decided he had endured enough. Since he knew nothing, yet, of his live shot's visual details, he decided to tweak the detective and give the crew in transmission a little entertainment, as if they needed it. "Tell me, Detective," asked Lentz in his same somber tone, "Do you think this was, uh, suicide?"

"No," the detective replied seriously, "we have, uh, ruled out that possibility pending further investigation."

# 13

Keep It Simple:
The Suitcase Theory of Packaging

Try to remember the last time you packed for a trip. Did you cram too many clothes into your suitcase? Did they come out wrinkled? And, when you opened the bag to grab an item, could you find it?

Apply the suitcase comparison to a television news package. Reporters overstuff stories, as well. *When a reporter puts too many twists or turns or facts into a story, he runs the risk of obscuring its message.*

Here's the disconcerting truth—if an average viewer takes away three facts from a television news segment, he's exceeded the legal limit. Three. As such, he prefers for stories to be digestible and uncomplicated. This doesn't mean dumbed-down or lazy. It means clear and straightforward. Try to make it easy for your viewer to find what he wants or needs.

# How Viewers Watch the News

In your mind, you may see yourself as a television news version of Cecil B. DeMille, but don't expect John and Mary Viewer to buy into it. They'll never give your work the same attention you do. A television news story is not a major motion picture. There is no curtain, no big screen, nor a big sound system. Television news audiences rarely dim the lights, and may not even be sitting down.

Sorry.

In many homes, the news blares from a box on the kitchen counter and competes with life's distractions. Your typical viewer listens more than watches. He comments more than listens. As your piece runs, he's making dinner, or talking on the phone, or doing homework with the kids, or working a crossword puzzle. Occasionally, when a story spikes his interest, he'll glance up. Even then, the segment will be halfway over, and he won't be taking notes.

## Change Places with the Viewer

A young reporter sent me a tape from a small market. He was twenty-three, still finding his way in a first job, and having problems with his reporting. "I feel overwhelmed," he wrote. Translated, that means he had a problem staying focused.

The reporter's tape included a late-news segment about a ruptured water main that cracked in subfreezing temperatures during a snowstorm. Barring complications, a public works crew would repair the damage before the next morning's rush hour, but the workmen did have a concern—that the water might freeze into a sheet of ice.

In a small town on a slow night, the break made big news. The broadcast producer asked for a live shot and a package insert. From looking at the reporter's tape, it's clear he tried hard with his assignment. If possible, he tried *too* hard.

The reporter and his photographer cut montages of running water accompanied by a symphony of jackhammers. In painstaking detail, he explained how workmen poked holes in the cement and used a special listening device to locate leaks. He filled the piece with monotonous facts, figures, and obscure details to the point that it looked less like a news story than an instructional video about street repair. If a viewer had watched closely, he might have been able to pass a civil service test.

All the reporter's problems trace back to one fundamental error. He never put himself in the place of people at home. He forgot that most of them didn't care about the specifics of urban repair. They simply wanted to know when Public Works would fix the break, and if they would need to find alternate routes for the morning commute. The reporter could have given his viewers that basic information in the first fifteen seconds of his live shot.

Then, if he had thought past the assignment sheet, he could have told a story to which anyone might relate—that on a very cold night this crew faced a mean, nasty job. Between their numb fingers, the frozen mud, and the struggle to keep flowing water from turning into sheets of ice, the reporter had plenty of material.

"Why didn't I think of that?" the kid asked later. Simple. We chalked it up to inexperience. He needed to take a figurative step back, look around, and trust his natural curiosity. But, at that stage of his career, this young reporter didn't have the confidence. He worried more about what he might miss than about what he might show, and crammed too many facts into a ninety-second package. He allowed fear, and his assignment, to confine him.

This is a common mistake. But the biggest obstacle to fixing it is recognizing it. When you find yourself in a similar circumstance, identify a single theme, character, or story line, and stay with it. Get to the point of the story. If the alphabet begins with "A" and finishes with "Z," don't feel obligated to detail all twenty-four letters in between.

The next time an assignment overwhelms you, that simple guideline may help.

# 14

## Report What You Find: *What Is* Will Always Be More Interesting Than What You Make Up

How many times have you gone to cover a flood, expected to find fearful citizens, and discovered them to be nonchalant, instead? Did you still try to do a story about fear, or did you adjust your approach? Reporters face this dilemma every day in all kinds of assignments. Due to time constraints or pressures from management, they ignore their own good instincts, and tailor stories to fit preconceived notions.

Have you heard of Guerneville, California? It's a free-spirited resort on the Russian River. For residents, life there might be perfect if not for the rainy season. Then, as winter storms blow in, this low-lying town inevitably becomes the first place in California to receive a flood warning—although, realistically, a press warning would be more appropriate.

In actuality, if Guerneville suffers any kind of a flood, it's less likely to come from the river than the media. At the first word of possible danger, reporters, cameras, and satellite trucks pour in, all urgently looking for high water of Biblical proportions.

It rarely materializes. Guerneville's founding mothers and fathers built the town with floods in mind. When the river rises, most of the supposed damage remains cosmetic, even if it does make good pictures. But, because journalists don't usually report their own overreactions, Guerneville's flood warnings still lead the news. Worse, some reporters go out of their way to find or conjure flood threats, even when they don't exist. I once overheard an interview similar to this:

REPORTER: "How worried are you about the high water?"

RESIDENT: "We're not worried at all. This town is built for high water. It only looks bad. At this level, I'm not worried about the river."

REPORTER: "What do you mean when you say it only looks bad?"

RESIDENT: "Oh, the water comes up over the banks and goes under the houses, but we've built them up, now, after the last flood."

REPORTER: "So what would you define as a bad flood?"

RESIDENT: "Back in 1995, that was bad. That was what they called a hundred-year flood. I had mud in my living room after that one. The place took half the summer drying out."

REPORTER: "Do you worry about that happening again?"

RESIDENT: "Oh sure, I always worry. Who wouldn't? Live it once, you'd worry, too."

REPORTER: "And if it floods this year?"

RESIDENT: "I don't even want to think about it. Bad news. Nobody wants that kind of mud again."

Sadly, the reporter used only the "bad news" part of his interview on the air. Later, he was insenstive enough to wonder why Guerneville residents treat the press so cynically.

It never occurred to him that, if he'd looked around and listened, he would have found a better angle in Guerneville's blasé attitude toward high water and the media. Such a story would have made the residents look hearty and brave. It would also have been the truth. And that's our job—telling the truth.

## Vandalized News Coverage

In 1995, our assignment editor spotted a newspaper item about how vandals broke into an eighth-grade computer lab in Middletown, a small community two hours north of San Francisco. Students were so angry that Martha Webster, editor of the *Middletown Times-Star,* invited them to write open letters to the vandal, promising to put them on the front page.

But, when she saw their grammar and spelling, Ms. Webster recognized a bigger story. *"You probly don't have the lightes ide how much truble you caused,"* wrote one pupil.

*"Dear Stpied delttect dume lame low lef. I don't think nobody can every forgive you,"* penned another.

Martha Webster couldn't believe her eyes. Many kids couldn't even spell the word "vandal." "It was galling," she said on camera— so galling that when she published those letters she didn't make a single correction. Parents, teachers, students, and ordinary citizens expressed outrage and embarrassment.

It sounded like a good story, so we headed to Middletown, and into the controversy, but it wasn't what it seemed. Unfortunately, when our desk man spied the item, he'd been in a hurry and never read all the way through. Instead, he faxed the article to photographer Randy Davis, who gave it to me when we rendezvoused in Middletown.

"Oh, no," I said after finishing it.

The letters had been published two years before. Not two days, two weeks, or two months, but *two years!* I called the station and suggested we might want to reconsider our coverage. "Do a piece, anyway," said our executive producer. "We like the spelling angle."

"This is a stretch," I told him.

"You stretch real well."

But the townspeople of Middletown disagreed. "It's sensationalism," lectured one parent.

"Why don't you find a real story somewhere else?" suggested another.

"This is old news," objected the school's principal. Randy and I agreed with her, but orders are orders. We still had to go through the motions of following up a two-year-old story we'd never covered.

Randy and I examined the possibilities. Could we do the piece without mentioning the two-year gap? Of course not. That wouldn't be ethical.

We began by visiting the newspaper, where we interviewed Ms. Webster. Then we waited for school to let out and found some of those eighth graders, who had since become tenth graders. We asked them to spell "vandal." Surprise, surprise—even after the hullabaloo of two years earlier, many of those kids still got the word wrong, but we needed more story to justify doing the piece.

## Exposing the Absent Villain

We found our angle by asking, "Why?" Middletown hadn't made the news again by accident. There had to be a motive behind this, and, if our assignment manager had read more, he would have caught the story's context.

A few days earlier, California State Assemblyman Steve Baldwin had given a speech in which he used Middletown's woes to make a case for stricter spelling standards in public schools.

Fair enough. Politicians manipulate facts and stories to their advantage every day. But Baldwin represented a district in Southern California, some three hundred miles away. We called his office. "Has Mr. Baldwin ever visited Middletown?"

"No," said a staff member.

"Has he spoken with any residents?"

"He is familiar with the case."

Baldwin's speech gave us a daily hook for the piece. Until we told them, Middletown residents never knew this politician had taken their old, dirty laundry and shaken it in front of the rest of the state.

Ultimately, this story wouldn't be about a vandal, or illiteracy, or a newspaper scandal, but about politics. When we put the facts to Middletown's citizens in those terms, they were happy to talk.

### MIDDLETOWN SPELLING
#### Summer 1997

[TRACK]
(over pictures of signs in town)
HERE IS A SIGN OF PROGRESS IN MIDDLETOWN.
THEY SPELLED "EXCELLENCE" RIGHT. AND
"ACADEMICS." ALONG WITH "STOP" AND "LIQUOR"
AND "DELI" AND "SALOON" . . . AND IF THAT
SOUNDS A LITTLE HARSH . . .

[SOT]
Wayne to a high-school boy: "SPELL 'VANDAL' FOR
ME."

Boy: "I couldn't spell 'vandal' for you."

Wayne: "OH COME ON. SPELL 'VANDAL.'"

Boy: "No."

[TRACK]
WE ASKED THAT QUESTION BECAUSE, TWO AND A
HALF YEARS AGO, A V-A-N-D-A-L BROKE INTO THE
MIDDLE SCHOOL AND WRECKED COMPUTERS. AT
THE TIME, ANGRY STUDENTS WROTE THE LOCAL
NEWSPAPER, WHICH PUBLISHED THOSE LETTERS.
BUT LOOK CLOSELY AT THE SPELLING. MANAGING
EDITOR MARTHA WEBSTER DECIDED TO PRINT THEM
AS WRITTEN.

[SOT]
Martha Webster: "It said there might be a problem
in the lower grades when eighth graders are having
this much difficulty with simple words."

[TRACK]
AND, DURING THE NEXT THREE WEEKS, SPELLING
BECAME THE BIGGEST NEWS IN TOWN, EVEN
AMONG THE KIDS WHO WROTE THOSE LETTERS.

[SOT]
Female student: "I read them and at first thought
they were a joke. They were really bad."

[STAND-UP]
DIG A LITTLE DEEPER, THOUGH, AND YOU'LL
DISCOVER THIS STORY ISN'T SO MUCH ABOUT
MIDDLETOWN AS IT IS ABOUT HOW CALIFORNIA
TEACHES THE ENGLISH LANGUAGE TO ITS
STUDENTS. SPECIFICALLY, SHOULD THE STATE

EMPHASIZE CREATIVITY INSTEAD OF GRAMMAR? OR
GRAMMAR INSTEAD OF CREATIVITY? IN SHORT, ONE
WORD, SPELLED . . .
P-O-L-I-T-I-C-S.

[TRACK]
(over file video of assemblyman)
. . . AS DEFINED BY ASSEMBLYMAN STEVE BALDWIN
OF RIVERSIDE, WHO REOPENED THE OLD WOUNDS
BY USING MIDDLETOWN'S LETTERS AS AMMUNITION
IN HIS FIGHT TO BRING BACK SPELLING TESTING TO
STATE SCHOOLS. HIS CAMPAIGN HAS NOT BEEN
PLAYING WELL HERE.

[SOT]
Mother in a car: "I think he needs to go and dig up
some new news somewhere else."

[SOT]
Wayne asks another high-school boy: "HOW DO
YOU SPELL 'VANDAL'?"

He answers: "V-A-N-D-E-L?"

[SOT]
A second mother: "It's sensationalism, that's what's
happening . . ."

[SOT]
Wayne continues with the kids, trying to get a
spelling of "vandal": "IS IT AN E-L OR AN A-L?"

Boy answers: "'E.' No. 'A'?"

[TRACK]
BUT, IF YOU SPEAK WITH THE LOCAL HIGH-SCHOOL
PRINCIPAL, WHERE MOST OF THOSE KIDS NOW GO
TO SCHOOL, A BETTER QUESTION WOULD BE HOW
TO SPELL "CHEAP SHOT."

[SOT]
Principal: "The state assemblyman has never been
here, never talked to me, never bothered to call
. . ."

[TRACK]
IF MR. BALDWIN HAD CALLED, HE MIGHT HAVE
LEARNED HOW EVEN THE NEWSWOMAN WHO BLEW
THE WHISTLE SAYS SKILLS HERE HAVE IMPROVED.
JUST LAST WEEK SHE RAN A STORY ABOUT A
MIDDLETOWN GIRL WHO SCORED IN THE TOP
TWENTY IN THE STATE SPELLING BEE . . .

[SOT]
Wayne to Martha Webster: "IS THERE A PROBLEM
HERE, NOW?"

Martha Webster: "I don't believe there is."

[TRACK]
FAIR ENOUGH, BUT IF THAT'S THE CASE, LET'S PUT
IT TO ONE, FINAL TEST. . .

[SOT]
Wayne asks a female student: "HOW DO YOU SPELL
'VANDAL'?"

She answers: "V-A-N-D-A-L?"

A second does the same: "V-A-N-D-A-L."

## Post Script

If television news were a perfect business, we wouldn't have had to struggle so hard to make that story, but I think we did right by Middletown. When the day began, its residents didn't like us. When it ended, we'd given them an opportunity to defend their reputation.

Ultimately, we made the best of a bad assignment by reporting what we found.

Part III

# PHILOSOPHY

# 15

## Craftsmanship and Restraint: Don't Mess with the Pope

The next time you come across a handcrafted wooden chair, take a few moments to examine it closely. Look at the lines. Whoever made that piece was a craftsman, a person so much in touch with his medium that he left no evidence of his sweat and toil. You won't notice the joints, the glue, or the nails. To the eye, they'll fit together as one.

For a finish carpenter, the work is about the furniture. For a television news reporter, the same standard applies. *His work should be about the stories.*

# The Benihana Trap

It's only natural that people in a performance medium want to show off their skills, but sometimes they overdo it. Those of us who write, report, shoot, or edit can easily fall into what I call the "Benihana trap."

Never heard of it? What about the restaurant chain by that same name? At Benihana of Tokyo, diners sit around a large grill while the chef conducts a cooking exhibition. He tosses knives and food, and chop, chop, chops his way through the courses. If you've had the experience, what do you most remember? Was it the meal or the chef?

I use this example because reporters and crews sometimes make a similar mistake when producing television news stories. They obscure their material by overwriting, overshooting, and overediting. In trying to impress coworkers or win awards, they forget their intended audience. It's the equivalent of making a chair to look at, rather than sit in.

When you study the most effective television news stories, you'll find that the craftsmanship looks effortless, if you notice it at all.

# Growing Pains and Confessions

This chapter is really about growing up and maturing as a reporter. Experience is the best teacher, and, after some of the stunts I pulled early in my career, it's amazing that I still work in this business. The worst was the time I single-handedly offended most of the Catholics in San Francisco.

## Never Try to Do a Funny Story About Religion or Politics

Of all the truisms in television news, remember this one—*viewers have thin skins about religion and politics. They rarely appreciate the humor.* It's a lesson I learned the hard way. In 1987, Pope John Paul II came to northern California as part of a national tour. For most of a week, KRON-TV followed the pontiff's every move. In the newsroom, we jokingly called it a "Pope-a-thon." His visit and our coverage culminated in a mass at Candlestick Park for sixty thousand devout Catholics. Amid tight security, both the crowd and the press arrived hours before dawn. I interviewed the faithful as they waited. Never have I seen people more content and devoted.

It had been such a historic day that we saved the field tapes for posterity. That was my first mistake. The second, a near-fatal one in terms of my career, came three months later. It began innocently enough. Actress Elizabeth Taylor had put her name on a new perfume, and, as part of a national promotional tour, she appeared at a local Macy's department store. The desk sent us to cover it.

Upon arrival, we couldn't believe the turnout. The line to see and meet Elizabeth Taylor extended through the entire cosmetics department, out the store's front door, and onto the sidewalk. Some fans had been there six hours, which was just as long as the Catholics had waited to see the pope at Candlestick. Moreover, it occurred to me that many of Ms. Taylor's devotees wore the same kind of blissful expressions.

I suppose by now you see where this is going. As a self-appointed observer and critic of the human condition, and as a reporter in search of the elusive different angle, I felt compelled to compare Elizabeth Taylor's visit to Macy's with that of the pope to Candlestick Park.

Ouch.

The idea was tasteless, insensitive, offensive, and stupid, but I thought it was brilliant. I intended it as a commentary about cosmetic values, but I forgot that viewers rarely appreciate sarcasm, particularly Catholics in reference to the pope. *Sometimes, it's much smarter for a reporter to suck it up and just do the obvious story.*

Back at the station, I ordered two graphics from the art department. The first showed a map of the pope's journey across America. The second detailed Ms. Taylor's perfume route. When our Catholic viewers saw those maps in the story, they did not appreciate my effort.

Next, I pulled out that file video, which had good stuff of emotional Catholics praising the pope and genuflecting at Candlestick Park. It seemed natural to contrast those shots with the scene at Macy's, where gleeful fans said similar things about Ms. Taylor, before practically throwing themselves at her feet. We cut back and forth—Macy's, Candlestick, Macy's, Candlestick, Macy's. Again, our viewers never quite caught the nuance.

But I saved the "best" for last. Looking through the file video, I also found a sequence of church officers sprinkling holy water on members of the Candlestick crowd. In the edit room, it cut perfectly with pictures of cosmetic saleswomen circulating through Macy's, spraying perfume—spritz, spritz, spritz.

Somehow the script cleared review, but the news director at that time was my old nemesis, Herb Dudnick. As the pope story ran, witnesses say, Herb shouted so loudly that the glass wall of his office bent visibly outward. They swear that Dudnick's face turned as red as a tomato, with veins bulging from his forehead.

In the newsroom, phones rang relentlessly for more than ninety minutes. The callers accused us of blasphemous heresy. If we'd lived in the Middle Ages, they would have burned me at the stake. Those callers swore they would never watch KRON-TV again.

Poor Herb Dudnick. He'd come to rebuild a news department and, by his definition, had begun to succeed. With his superior coverage of the pope's visit, Herb had won viewers. Then I did my story, and shooed away most of the Catholics in one minute and fifty-three seconds.

After the piece aired, Herb Dudnick rushed to the edit bay. In what must have been an effort to turn back the clock, he bulk erased the tape. And yet, for unexplained reasons, the fearsome Herb Dudnick did not fire or even suspend me. No—in some ways, the punishment was worse. Herb relegated me to the medical beat, where a reporter with bad judgment couldn't possibly do more damage. Or so it seemed.

But the AIDS epidemic was making big news at that time, and my very first story dealt with the development of a female condom. It required me to say the word "vagina" while sitting live on set. Well, after the pope fiasco, I was such a nervous wreck that, when it came time to say the word, I began to stutter. "V-V-V-V-V- . . ." I couldn't get it out. "V-V-V—Vagina!"

In retrospect, it is clear that Herb Dudnick was a good and patient man. Despite his temper, Herb Dudnick practiced restraint as a manager, and also as a human being. A few years later, he even recommended me for a job.

I guess he never mentioned the pope.

# 16

## A Few Thoughts About Writing

Check that. I have "a few" thoughts about writing in the same way General Motors makes "a few" cars. In television news reporting, writing isn't everything, but it comes close. Good writing marries words with pictures, sounds, interviews, and concepts. With skillful writing, a reporter can take marginal material and breathe life into it. With bad writing, he'll take wonderful material and kill it.

## If You Don't Like the Way You Sound . . .

If you already work in television news, you probably have a good or at least decent speaking voice, but that doesn't guarantee you like the way you sound. You wouldn't be the first to fret about breathing, delivery, or inflection, never realizing that your problems have less to do with elocution than the words you choose. *If you want to come across as an approachable, believable person on television, write the way you speak.*

## The News Dialect

People undergo strange transformations when they get behind a microphone. Their voices drop deeper. They utter words and phrases they would never use in normal conversation:

> SHOCKING DEVELOPMENT
> AN IRONIC NEW TWIST
> THE VERY LATEST
> COMPLETELY DESTROYED
> A HORRIBLE TRAGEDY
> LIVE TEAM COVERAGE

Do BOOKS FLY OFF SHELVES because they have wings? Who is MOTHER NATURE? Is she related to FATHER TIME? What is a MAKESHIFT MEMORIAL? When an agency BEEFS UP SECURITY, does it put cattle by the door? When SHOTS RANG OUT, did they play a tune? When EMERGENCY CREWS RACED TO THE SCENE, did one of them receive a checkered flag?

What's going on here? Such reflexive writing puts invisible barriers between news people and an already skeptical public. It doesn't sound real. Who do we think we're fooling? If we don't communicate that way in real life, why do we do it on the air? When, for instance, was the last time you sat down to dinner and heard your spouse announce, "Next up, the pot roast." And what if that pot roast turned out burned? Obviously, "Something went terribly wrong."

## Active, Not Passive

Speaking of wrong, find the flaw in this sentence:

> HE WAS SHOT.

We hear the verb SHOT, but never learn who pulled the trigger.
   Here's a possibility, however:

> SOMEONE WHO DOESN'T LIKE PASSIVE VOICE SHOT
> HIM.

To write actively, identify the subject first. State what he, she, or it did, does, or will do, and to what or whom. Passive-voice sentences usually don't tell a complete story. We write them because we're in a hurry, or lazy, or don't have all the facts. You can't hope to adequately replace those absent facts with a bad habit.

## Non-Descriptive Linking Verbs

Be wary of linking verbs such as:

> IS
> ARE
> WAS
> WERE

When you see them in your copy, challenge yourself to find more descriptive action verbs—but, if you have to try too hard, forget it. If William Shakespeare used an occasional "is" in his copy (and he did), we may do so, too.

## Elocution Convolutions

This is another symptom of how television news people complicate their copy. Instead of writing simple sentences, writers lapse into parenthetical phrases or use big words, and more of them than they need. Of an embattled congressman, a reporter might write:

CONGRESSMAN JOHN DOE, MARRIED TO THE SAME
WOMAN FOR THIRTY-FIVE YEARS, SAYS HE'S NEVER
HAD AN AFFAIR WITH AN INTERN.

Would you speak like that to a friend? No wonder you might stumble while saying it. Why not use simple, short, declarative sentences?

THE CONGRESSMAN HAS BEEN MARRIED TO THE
SAME WOMAN FOR THIRTY-FIVE YEARS. HE SAYS HE
WOULD NEVER CHEAT ON HER.

While we're on the subject of sentences, here's a nomination for the most ridiculous of all time. It comes from a newscast in Sacramento, California:

THE OBVIOUS CONCLUSION AND BOTTOM LINE
WAS THAT SHE WAS A PARTICIPANT IN HER OWN
DEATH.

Or, to put it another way:

SHE KILLED HERSELF.

And that writer killed the story.

## Mixed Metaphors

Don't get overly fancy with your writing. After a certain point, it can only cause trouble.

I heard one such example following the September 11 terrorist attacks. You may recall how the FAA had temporarily grounded airplane charter companies because of security concerns. In the Denver market, one reporter went to a local airport for an economic impact story. THEY'RE TAKING ON WATER AND IN DANGER OF SINKING, he wrote of one charter firm. Nice try. Had that company owned a seaplane, his line might have been acceptable.

## ... But Enough Nitpicking

Hopefully, now you'll look more closely at the words you choose. There are some excellent books on the subject. Read *Writing Broadcast News—Shorter, Sharper, Stronger* by Mervin Block. If you fancy yourself a good writer, Mervin will humble you, much as he did me while helping to edit this project.

At least he was funny about it, most of the time.

# Using Sound

Writing well for television news requires more than words. If this is, in fact, a visceral medium, viewers must also feel, sense, and hear. To achieve that, writers need to learn to use sound effectively.

## Write from Point to Point

By now, you've read a few of my scripts, and you might have noticed that I don't usually write more than two or three sentences before inserting a piece of sound. I learned the style from a photographer. This shouldn't surprise you. In entry-level markets particularly, some photographers are more qualified to report than the reporters with whom they work. Many of these shooters edit their own stories and bring a sense of ownership to them. In such environments, no self-respecting photographer will let a reporter ruin a piece. Ideally, they work as a team.

Such was my relationship with Kerry McGee, a classmate at the University of Missouri who, after graduation, joined our staff at WAVE-TV in Louisville. We worked together almost every day, and

McGee would pester me about writing long-winded scripts. "You're a vocal narcissist," he would taunt, and it was true. I had a misguided love affair with my own voice. To me it sounded wonderful, even if nobody else thought so.

McGee could be merciless. The man shot pictures for a living but wielded a quick, sharp pencil. If he didn't like a script, he pushed for revisions, right up to deadlines. "What's this?" he would scold. "That's wall-to-wall words. Are we doing radio, here?"

Thanks to Kerry McGee, I have a sense of pacing that survives to this day. Short narrative tracks lead into sound bites or bits of sound, and then new tracks continue the thoughts, as if in a dialogue.

Here is a section of script that blends narrative tracks with sound bites and snippets of natural sound. The piece was a profile of the Fresno High School Warriors, who, in 1992, had lost thirty-one consecutive football games:

**0-31**
**September 1992**

[SOT]
(tight shot: wrapping athletic tape around an ankle)

[TRACK]
IN A WORLD OF BONE, SINEW, STRENGTH, AND
WILLPOWER, THERE IS NOTHING MORE BAFFLING
THAN THAT STRING OF EVENTS KNOWN AS A
"STREAK."

[SOT]
(two guys slap shoulder pads)

[TRACK]
STREAKS DEFY LOGIC . . .

[SOT]
Player: "Superstition is superstition . . ."

[TRACK]
THEY TAKE ON LIVES . . .

[SOT]
Wayne: "HOW MANY TIMES HAVE YOU LOST,
NOW?"

Second player: "I don't know. You'll have to ask
someone else . . ."

[TRACK]
SOME WOULD SAY STREAKS HAVE WILLS OF THEIR
OWN . . .

[SOT]
Players in huddle: "We want a win! Pride!"

[TRACK]
FOR A FOOTBALL TEAM, A STREAK CAN BE THE
BEST OF FRIENDS, OR THE WORST OF ENEMIES . . .

[SOT]
(team crashes through barrier and takes field)

[TRACK]
NO ONE KNOWS BETTER THAN THE WARRIORS OF
FRESNO HIGH SCHOOL . . .

[SOT]
First player: "It's more than just a game. By now,
we have to redeem ourselves as human beings . . ."

## Writing Seamless Sound

Did you notice the seamless transitions in that script? It's the
same effect you sometimes get while riding a train. When passing
over rough sections of track, you notice every junction of every
rail. But, when you travel on a good stretch of track, it's a smooth
trip, and you don't feel the connections at all. Television news stories link sections, too, but they ride on narration and sound instead of rails.

## Sound That Reads Well on Paper
## Doesn't Always Play Well on Tape

Beware that what looks good on paper doesn't always translate into
good television. Writing a seamless script is more complicated.

Among the more common mistakes: reporters or editors force
sound bites into their stories. A reporter may know what a person
said or means because he's seen the tape three or four times, but the
audience doesn't have the same advantage. If a sound bite comes
unexpectedly or is too short, or if viewers don't hear it clearly, then
it's an unwanted distraction from the story—a bump in the track
that raises more questions than it answers.

## Find the Clean Edit Point

Edit your sound bites at the cleanest, most natural points, even if it
means sacrificing a few extra seconds. When possible, avoid entering or exiting a sound bite in mid-clause or mid-sentence. It's always better to let your subjects finish their own thoughts. Our
viewers are suspicious enough already.

## Adjust Your Script and Inflection to Match the Sound Bite

With any piece of sound, use your writing and vocal inflection to smooth the transition. Listen to the sound bite in your mind before reading the accompanying track. Try to match or complement the sound bite's energy level. If you don't like the fit, return to the booth to read it again. Don't be ashamed of retakes. My good friend and regular editor James Sudweeks has become so used to them that he always keeps a second tracking tape next to his playback machine.

## Match the Background Sounds

Sudweeks—or "Suds," as we call him—is a stickler with sound, and a master at blending two audio channels into one. He pays particular attention to noises in the background. They can wreak havoc on seamless editing.

Let's say you have an interview on a busy street with a jackhammer audible in the distance. Common sense dictates that this interview won't cut cleanly with another recorded in an empty room. The jackhammer, and any other changes, will be distracting, if not counterproductive.

As a standard practice, try to conduct your interviews in a neutral audio environment, and remember to record a few seconds of room tone or ambient sound before leaving. Guys like Suds will thank you later.

Finally, you might wonder why I consider such technical concerns to be a part of writing. Well, the more you know about the technical process, the better you'll be able to work with a story's limitations or potential. As the writer, you're the person who maps it out on paper.

# In Every Story, Establish and Maintain a Rhythm

When you listen to people in conversation, you'll note that their natural vocal tones and rhythms change with the time, place, and circumstance. Try to find your own appropriate tone and rhythm, too. Give your stories a musicality and a beat. Listen for it as you write. Adapt it to each piece. Sad stories may be slower. Happier ones may be faster.

Almost every story should have such an internal metronome, but don't force an inappropriate tempo. Do not, for example, cut a flashy, fast-paced open for material that can't sustain such an energy level. Reporters commonly make this mistake when trying to liven up dry stories. They hope to give a piece momentum, but, in fact, when they promise a pace they can't deliver, the rest of a package feels slow by comparison.

## The Rule of Threes

*We came, we saw, we conquered.*

Do you hear the rhythm in that sentence? When we group words or phrases into threes, they sound more compelling and dramatic. *We're born, we live, we die.*

Threes also work when writing television news. Here is the open to a piece from the day a fourteen-year-old boy shot his classmates at Santana High School near San Diego, California:

> [TRACK]
> THE LUCKY ONES WALKED OUT OF SANTANA HIGH
> SCHOOL THIS MORNING. THEY WERE GRATEFUL NOT
> TO BE LEAVING ON GURNEYS . . .
> OR IN WHEELCHAIRS . . .
> OR BY HELICOPTER, AFTER ONE OF THEIR OWN

```
TOOK A TWENTY-TWO-CALIBER HANDGUN AND
OPENED FIRE IN A RESTROOM.
```

Do you hear the threes? GURNEYS—WHEELCHAIRS—HELICOPTER.

Here is another example, from a story about a cat named Stanley. In 2001, he made national news by habitually climbing a neighborhood power pole and staying there for days on end:

```
[TRACK]
IN THE LIFESPAN OF ANY STREET, THERE ARE BUSY
DAYS . . .
THERE ARE QUIET DAYS . . .
AND, ON BOWLING GREEN STREET IN SAN
LEANDRO, THERE ARE STANLEY DAYS.
```

Try reading it aloud until you hear the rhythm.

## Change the Cadence

As useful as threes can be, they aren't the only rhythm in the English language. When overused, threes become repetitious and ineffective, so pick your spots. Don't put threes in every piece, and alter the cadence when you do. Sprinkle in a few ones or twos for contrast.

Below you'll find a section of script that uses threes in combination with a pair of twos. Again, read it aloud and listen to the cadence:

```
[TRACK]
IF THE HIGHWAY TO HADES HAS AN EARTHLY
OPPOSITE, THIS MAY BE THE PLACE. THE COLDER
THE TEMPERATURES, THE HOTTER THE TEMPERS . . .
```

The rhythm words are:

- HADES, OPPOSITE, and PLACE accent the threes.
- COLDER and TEMPERATURES, paired with HOTTER and TEMPERS, accent the twos.

## It Takes Time and Practice

To find rhythm in your writing, listen to the lyrics of your favorite songs. Read poetry. Expose yourself to different word treatments. Experiment. Rent a movie in which a narrator moves the plot forward.

Morgan Freeman does a wonderful job in *The Shawshank Redemption*. Listen to him work the words. There's no rush, no hurry. The pace is perfect. You'll hear another good narration from Robert Redford in *A River Runs Through It*. His read at the end is a classic in cadence and simplicity.

It might help if you copy the words, play the movies back, and read along with them. Or do the same with some well-written television news stories. When you match your voice to those of the masters, the quality can be catching.

# 17

---

## Seek the Simple Truths

---

In television news, reporters write differently than in any other
medium.

They write to be heard. They write parallel with pictures. A well-
written story takes viewers beyond the superficial. The best pieces
leave lifelong impressions.

Greg Lyon, a reporter at KRON-TV, once did a story about hard
economic times for California's salmon fishermen. His photogra-
pher/editor, Lou D'Aria, wanted to use a low, long-lens shot of a
seagull pecking at a morsel of food between the planks of a pier.
That darn bird simply wouldn't give up. Peck, peck, peck.

Greg tortured himself trying to find a line to fit the shot. He
wrote a few words and ripped them up. Then he tried another line
and tore that up, too. This continued for a while. We'll never know

how many trees Greg killed, but I'll remember the line for which they died:

> [TRACK]
> THE LIVING IS WHERE THEY FIND IT.

Those were seven choice words—short, simple, and descriptive. They spoke beyond the picture.

At about the same time, John Hart of NBC News wrote another telling line. In a piece about illegal immigrants slipping across America's southern borders, Hart described the frustrations of customs officials. He compared their job to that of someone trying to catch . . .

> [TRACK]
> PEBBLES IN AN AVALANCHE.

Quite an image, isn't it?

Watch Steve Hartman's work at CBS News. In a story at the Grand National Rodeo, he wrote of an overmatched cowboy needing . . .

> [TRACK]
> THE RIDE OF HIS LIFE, THE FOURTH NIGHT IN A
> ROW.

With one simple line, Steve described hope and virtual impossibility.

Hartman transcends journalism. "But sometimes I feel like such an imposter," he likes to say. Hardly. Steve is an old soul, wise beyond his years, and he brings it to his work.

## Simple Truths

All three of those lines speak to simple truths. Instead of stating the obvious, they enable a viewer to find deeper, universal meanings in stories. It's much the same as leading a person to a door and then letting him step though to make a discovery himself. Usually, he appreciates it more that way.

Simple truths are elusive. They're details or sentiments so obvious, sometimes, that we may fail to recognize them. Where, for example, is the simple truth in a forest? Is it the trees? Or the silence?

Where is the simple truth in an urban murder?

> [TRACK]
> IN OAKLAND, THEY'RE NOTING THE YEAR'S
> NINETIETH HOMICIDE VICTIM MORE FOR HIS
> NUMBER THAN HIS NAME.

Later, we learned that number ninety's name was McKinley Williams, a thirty-three-year-old construction worker with two children. He'd been playing basketball before being shot, and still wore his gym clothes. Those would have been good details, but, in the absence of them, *we described intangibles.* I didn't need a press release or a fact check to write that line. That kind of simple truth comes from connecting your humanity with your material.

## Writing at the Highest Level

In this book, I've told you what I regard to be the essentials for telling a memorable narrative story. We've looked at the basics—beginnings, middles, endings, main characters, and story lines. But, when you frame them in simple truths, you rise to the highest levels of our calling. Early on, I wrote about looking for stories of life in the stories we cover every day. Simple truths cut to the heart of that.

## The Grateful Deadhead

Simple truths can appear anywhere in stories, and may take the form of a small observation.

In 1997, we spent a day with the late Dick Latvala, whose name means a great deal to fans of the Grateful Dead. Thirty years earlier, he'd chucked his job as a mailman and dropped out of regular society to become, as he described it, "a full-on, Deadhead hippie freak." Dick spent years following the Dead around America, taping their concerts. Eventually, when the band needed an archivist, his dedication paid off. The Grateful Dead hired Dick:

> [TRACK]
> FOR DICK, THE DEAD BECAME A LIVING . . .

## Think It, Write It

That simple truth worked as a play on words. It came to me in a moment of relaxed clarity. When writing, you cannot summon such a state. It arrives, but only when you're ready to receive it.

If you're having a hard time with inspiration, help the muse along. I once asked Devorah Major, the poet laureate of San Francisco, how she teaches children to write metaphors. "You use your senses and comparative thinking," she said. "Look at a pink sunset. Of what would the color remind you? Cotton candy. What would it sound like? Quiet. If the pink color had an emotion, what would it be? Calm. It leads to a calm, cotton candy sunset."

# Listen to Your Inner Voice:
# The World's Newest Oldest Human

Chris Mortensen took 115 years to become a household name. By then, he had outlived his wives, his children, and most of his grandchildren. Finally, after the death of a woman in France, he ascended to the title of World's Oldest Person. The next day, we did a report about him.

Mr. Mortensen, we soon learned, was blind and almost deaf. At 115 years old, he lived in one small room in a retirement home. His worldly possessions had dwindled until they filled only a chest of drawers. Being the newly recognized World's Oldest Person did not impress him. In the interview, Chris Mortensen didn't say much.

On our way back to the car I commented to the photographer, "If someone hangs around long enough, I suppose he earns the title by default." We chuckled about that, but, later, the thought led to an opening line, which we used over pictures of a tired old man in a wheelchair:

> [TRACK]
> THERE ARE SOME TITLES FOR WHICH WE WORK,
> OTHERS FOR WHICH WE ASPIRE, AND, SOMETIMES,
> TITLES FIND US.
> FOR CHRIS MORTENSEN OF SAN RAFAEL, THE LAST
> OF THOSE THREE HAS HAPPENED, THOUGH, AT 115
> YEARS OLD, TITLES DON'T MUCH IMPRESS HIM.

## Experience the Story

Ernest Hemingway used to say that, before expressing an idea, a writer must free himself by experiencing it. Live the moment fully.

Neil Armstrong certainly did so when he set foot on the moon. "That's one small step for a man—one giant leap for mankind," he said. Armstrong wasn't a great writer, but no one ever spoke wiser, simpler, and more truthful words.

It doesn't take a moonwalk to achieve that kind of clarity. In 2001, a forest fire closed forty miles of Interstate 80 between Sacramento, California, and Reno, Nevada. Somewhere in the middle, photographer Stan Wong and I stopped to take pictures. For a few minutes, we stood alone on the yellow line—just us, the empty highway, the terrain, and the distant smoke. Surrounded by that rugged country, the asphalt looked unnatural. I reflected how men had exercised their will by cutting through the Sierra Nevada, and about the fact that, for one day, at least, the mountains claimed it back. A personal observation became a factual line of track:

[TRACK]
ALTHOUGH MEN BUILT INTERSTATE 80, FOR NOW,
NATURE WILL DECIDE WHEN THEY USE IT . . .

## The Zone

Is there a sport at which you're exceptionally good? Do you play a musical instrument? If either is the case, you may have visited that place called "the zone." It's where you forget about mechanics and lose yourself in the moment. Simple truths work the same way.

Once we did a piece about a rookie baseball league for little boys. During a lull in the game, photographer Michael Clark rolled tape of one kid waiting at the plate with a bat on his shoulder. Seemingly out of nowhere, the youngster blew a wad of gum into a head-sized bubble. Then it popped:

[TRACK]
. . . AT THIS LEVEL, EVEN THE INACTION IS ACTION-
PACKED.

As the moment happened, I scribbled the line into a notebook. Later, it worked for the piece.

# Finding A Simple Truth Theme: "Things to Remember"

Often, our most challenging stories become some of our best. They force us to demand more of ourselves, particularly when trying to write up to extraordinary material. At such times, self-doubt may, in fact, make you a better writer.

I had one of those projects on a Thursday night in 1991. Five days earlier, the Oakland Hills had caught fire, burning thousands of homes. Most of us working in the San Francisco Bay area had covered other big disasters, including the Loma Prieta Earthquake of 1989, but inch for inch, block by block, victim by victim, few of us ever saw a more devastating force than the Oakland Hills firestorm.

It began on a Sunday afternoon, with a charcoal cloud covering the eastern hills. In a few hours, wind-driven flames consumed entire neighborhoods. Many of the people who lost their homes had only minutes to escape. They left behind pets, papers, photographs, and memories.

The rest of that week, we covered the aftermath. Late on Thursday, Milt Weiss, KGO-TV's news director at the time, asked for what he called "a think piece." "We'll run it tomorrow," he said. I appreciated Milt's confidence, but after five days of coverage it seemed we'd shown and said all we could about the fire. More daunting, Milt wanted the segment to fill three or four minutes.

I began by reviewing the week's stories. Our staff had done some fine work, and several pieces stood out. Among them, we profiled Oakland fireman Gary Paccini, who lost his own house while helping to save seven others. In another story we profiled local families who opened their doors to fire victims. Loren and Maureen Bybee, for example, adopted a family of seven.

I must have looked through every newscast, searching for stories, pictures, interviews, and spontaneous moments. Then I went back to the field tapes, hoping for new material we might have over-looked, or not had time to use.

Collectively, they made a storytelling gold mine, but such rich-ness came with a price. There was too much material. I tried every possible way to jumpstart a script, including compiling a list of words from a thesaurus, but I couldn't make headway in the writ-ing. After a week of doing and watching fire stories, every word and phrase sounded overstated or trite.

Two hours after sitting down to write, my computer screen had just as many words as when I started—none.

I thought about the fire victims who would see this segment. Who was I to speak for them? My own house hadn't been touched. I felt guilty about it. How could anyone else appreciate what those people had endured? Impossible. If a person wasn't a victim, it made him an outsider.

The concept struck a chord. It almost felt original. "That's the first clear thought you've had all night," I told myself, and wrote it down:

> NO ONE CAN APPRECIATE WHAT THESE PEOPLE ARE
> GOING THROUGH, UNLESS THEY HAVE DONE SO
> THEMSELVES . . .

I looked at the numbers of planes and fire trucks, the crews, and the dollars spent. In spite of our best men and machines, the fire had run us over:

> EVEN WITH ALL OUR TECHNOLOGY, THERE WAS
> NOTHING WE COULD DO . . .

I reflected on the loss of life and property. Earlier in the week we had used a shot of firemen poking through rubble and finding what appeared to be human remains. I connected that with another shot, of a burned doll inside a little girl's hope chest:

> THERE ARE SOME THINGS THESE PEOPLE HAVE LOST
> THEY HAVEN'T EVEN THOUGHT OF YET . . .
> IT'S THE STUFF THAT TRIGGERS MEMORIES.

The line dealt with feeling overwhelmed. Anyone who has suffered a loss knows how, for days, weeks, and years after, forgotten details resurface.

From those three thoughts, the theme began to find itself. It became a story of observational details and memories:

## THINGS TO REMEMBER
### August 1991

[TRACK]
FROM THE BEGINNING, WE KNEW THIS WAS
DIFFERENT . . . AS IF WHAT HAD BEEN A QUIET FIRE
SEASON DECIDED TO MAKE UP FOR LOST TIME, ALL
AT ONCE.
FROM ACROSS THE BAY IN SAN FRANCISCO, THIS
BILLOWING CHARCOAL SKY LOOKED OMINOUS. IN
THE EAST BAY HILLS, IT WAS OVERWHELMING . . .

[SOT]
Woman cries: "My home, my home."
(full sound and pictures of flames)

[TRACK]
FOR THOSE WHO LIVED THROUGH IT, THESE SIGHTS

AND SOUNDS ARE SEARED INTO MEMORY.
THE FUTILITY OF A GARDEN HOSE . . .

[SOT]
(man tries to save his roof with a hose)
Neighbor shouts: "Get away!"

[TRACK]
THE FURY OF THE WIND . . .

[SOT]
(wind and flames crackle; fire blows across highway)

[TRACK]
AND, FINALLY, THE REALIZATION THAT, EVEN WITH
ALL OUR TECHNOLOGY, THERE WAS NOTHING WE
COULD DO.

[SOT]
(plane drops fire retardant)

[TRACK]
THROUGH A LONG AFTERNOON AND ON INTO
EVENING, THOUSANDS OF HOMES BURNED.

[SOT]
(natural sound as the camera drives past several
burning homes; the sequence continues with more
houses; we dissolve into shots of the fire at sunset,
and then night)

[TRACK]
IF WE FOUND COMFORT IN THE DARKNESS, IT CAME
FROM WHAT WE COULDN'T SEE . . .

[SOT]
(we see a fleeing family loading a car)
The woman gasps: "Oh, dear God."

[TRACK]
IF WE FELT ANGER, IT CAME FROM WHAT WE
COULDN'T CONTROL . . .

[SOT]
(a distraught man puts his head in his hands)

[TRACK]
AND, IN THE SHELTERS ALL THAT NIGHT, IF WE
KNEW FEAR, IT CAME FROM WHAT WE DID NOT
KNOW . . .

[SOT]
Woman: "You don't know if you'll ever see your
home again. Maybe it isn't a palace to someone
else, but it is to me. It's all I have. This is ripping
out my heart . . ."

[SOT]
(pictures from sunrise, the morning after, show
people and ruins; we hear the trickling sound of
water pouring down a storm drain.)

[TRACK]
NO ONE CAN APPRECIATE WHAT THESE PEOPLE ARE
GOING THROUGH UNLESS THEY HAVE DONE SO
THEMSELVES. THEY HAVE LOST FRIENDS AND
FAMILY, SOMETIMES WITHOUT A TRACE.

[SOT]
(we see a long-lens shot of firemen looking for
human remains in a charred house)

[TRACK]
THEY HAVE LOST SECURITY . . .

[SOT]
(another long-lens shot: a mother and son walk
away, carrying suitcases.)

[TRACK]
THERE ARE SOME THINGS THESE PEOPLE HAVE LOST
THAT THEY HAVEN'T EVEN THOUGHT OF YET. SOME
WILL SAY THEY'RE ONLY OBJECTS, BUT IT'S THE
STUFF THAT TRIGGERS MEMORIES. THE FIRE
REDUCED THEM ALL TO BURNSCAPE.

[SOT]
(we talk to a little girl)
Wayne asks if she's seen her house: "No, I couldn't
look. I didn't want to go."

[SOT]
(we dissolve to pictures of rescue crews removing a
burned cat from beneath wreckage; the cat meows)

[TRACK]
THERE ARE NO SILVER LININGS IN A STORY LIKE
THIS, BUT, FOR THOSE WHO LOOK, THERE CAN BE
HOPE AND INSPIRATION.
FOR EVERY PERSON MISSING A PET, THERE IS THIS
SIAMESE WHO HAS A NEW NAME—PELE, AFTER THE

HAWAIIAN GODDESS OF FIRE. SHE'S GOING TO BE
ALL RIGHT . . .

[SOT]
(we dissolve to video of fireman Gary Paccini as he
surveys his burned-down house)

[TRACK]
FOR THOSE WHO BELIEVE IN HONOR AND DUTY,
THERE IS OAKLAND FIREMAN GARY PACCINI, WHO
HELPED RESCUE SEVEN HOMES, BUT RETURNED TO
FIND HIS OWN HAD TURNED TO DUST . . .

[SOT]
Gary: "I was already committed where we
were . . ."

[TRACK]
AND THEN THERE'S THE GOODNESS OF HUMAN
SPIRIT. THE VOLUNTEERS WHO, WHEN NEEDED,
GAVE OF THEMSELVES . . .

[SOT]
(we hear a crying baby and see a crowded living
room.)

[TRACK]
. . . PEOPLE LIKE LOREN AND MAUREEN BYBEE,
WHO OPENED THEIR HOME TO STRANGERS, THE
SILVA FAMILY . . . HENRY AND JACQUELINE AND
THEIR FIVE KIDS.

[SOT]
Wayne asks Maureen what she got out of this: "You
feel good about yourself. What you put out you get
back, and sevenfold."

[SOT]
(helicopter sound—an aerial shot looks down upon
a landscape of burned homes)

[TRACK]
TWO YEARS AGO, WE SURVIVED AN EARTHQUAKE.
THEN CAME THIS.
NATURE HAS SHAKEN US.
SHE HAS BURNED US.
BUT SHE HAS NOT BROKEN US.

## Simple Truths as Endings

Here is a simple truth we used as an ending. Every year, hundreds if
not thousands of people ask professional sports teams if they may
sing the national anthem before a game. In 1991 the Oakland Athletics held an open tryout. Dozens of hopefuls auditioned.

For reporters and photographers who covered this event, the experience was, in a word, excruciating. To succeed at singing the national anthem, a person must nail that high note in "O'er the land
of the free . . ." Some squeaked it. Others screeched it. Most who
tried never reached it.

Adding to our pain, the Athletics piped those singers through an
ear-splittingly loud public address system. With every new performer, we began to anticipate the horrible sound. We cringed; we
cowered; we covered our ears; we ground and teeth and grimaced.
"Freeeeeeeeeeeeeeeee!"

But at least I took something away from the experience—this line:

    [TRACK]
    . . . THE NATIONAL ANTHEM
    BELONGS TO ALL OF US. BUT,
    IN THIS LAND OF THE . . .

    [SOT]
    A montage of auditioners missing the high note in
    "free," and people holding their ears:
    "Free/Freeeee/Freee . . ."

    [TRACK]
    . . . ONLY THE BRAVEST SHOULD TRY TO SING IT.

# 18

## Look Beyond the Superficial: Sometimes, Stories Can Be About Something Else

Anyone who leads police on a 110-mile car chase must imagine he has a good reason. He's either running away from something, or to it.

Curious yet? Kevin Keeshan, my news director at KGO-TV, certainly was. When he learned we'd purchased freelance video of such a pursuit and the subsequent arrest, he pushed the story my way.

"Something's going on with this," Keeshan said.

I wasn't too keen on the idea. "It was a car chase."

"No. It was 110-mile car chase. Sometimes, we have to do this stuff." He wondered if there might be more to the story.

I still didn't care much for it. Nobody had gotten hurt. Police had the suspect in jail. And, most irritating for me or any journalist, we suffered from a dearth of information. The arresting officers had worked late, gone home, and not yet filed reports. Aside from a few minutes of shaky, grainy stringer video and one paragraph of wire copy, we knew nothing. But even when an assignment doesn't thrill you, motivate yourself to work it. My motivation, that particular day, came from trying to prove the boss wrong.

In the chase, the suspect had led police through five counties and more than a dozen small cities. I began by telephoning detectives in every one of them. Nobody said much. Cops generally confirm only as much as you know, and then maybe tell a little more.

But, when a reporter spends three hours asking questions, one piece of information leads to another. If he's lucky, the puzzle pieces click together and a picture emerges. That's what happened with this story.

One detective disclosed that the suspect had been driving a stolen green Ford Explorer. Then a second officer, in another city, boasted that his own department's auto theft task force had played a leading role in the arrest.

"But the chase began thirty miles south of you, in San Jose," I mentioned.

"It was a stakeout."

"A stolen car stakeout?"

"Can't say."

"But that's a good guess?"

"That's a good guess. And I've told you too much already."

I called a third detective in another city. "So, we know it was a stolen truck, but who owned it?"

"Peninsula Ford," he said casually.

Bingo. He'd opened the door. I could call the dealer, ask questions, and, most important, extract firsthand information from someone who wasn't a police officer. I rang Peninsula Ford and spoke with the sales manager, Elliott Negron. "Oh yeah, that's our truck for sure," he said. "I knew it when I saw it on the news."

"Were you surprised?"

"We already knew something was going down."

"And why is that?"

Negron explained that the Explorer had disappeared two nights earlier. "The thieves cracked the key out of the lock box and drove it off the lot."

"That has to be maddening."

"We're getting used to it," he said. "Local dealerships have lost twenty cars in the last month."

"Dealerships? As in, more than one?"

"You don't know about this?"

With that, the puzzle began to take shape. No wonder police hadn't said much. "So, when they stopped that suspect in your truck last night . . ."

"Yeah," finished Negron. "They busted a stolen car ring."

And, suddenly, the story wasn't about just a car chase anymore. "Can you clear something up?" I asked. "Why did the chase begin thirty miles south, in San Jose?"

"That's the other part of this. I have a mechanic with sharp eyes."

"Tell me more."

"Well, he knew about the thefts. Everybody did." Negron told how thieves had stolen so many cars from so many dealers that their "inventory" exceeded both manpower and storage space. Sometimes they would heist a car, leave it in the neighborhood, and pick it up later.

Enter Negron's mechanic, who took a lunchtime walk and spotted what looked like a new Chevrolet sitting on a side street. He went back and told Negron, who called the police, who confirmed the car as stolen. Inside its glove box they found a receipt from a San Jose hotel. Detectives drove down, looked around, and found a fleet of stolen cars in the parking lot. They staked the place out, and later that night, when the bad guys returned, our 110-mile car chase began.

It was basic connect-the-dots reporting, but the day reminded me how stories can have layers of relevance, and speak to viewers on several interest levels. What began as a one-line story about a 110-mile chase became a tale of stolen cars, persistent cops, and, best of all, a little guy, the mechanic, who set the events in motion. If we wanted to push the piece further, we could add the story of a twenty-seven-year-old suspect who'd bounced in and out of jail since age eighteen because of a drug habit.

That's a little something for everyone. It would appear that my news director had darn good instincts.

## Look at the Bigger Picture: Galaxy 4

Do you remember a communications satellite called Galaxy 4? In 1998, it broke, interrupting a large percentage of America's pagers and wireless communications. Until then, most Americans took their pagers and e-mails for granted, but Galaxy 4 changed that. Its loss of signal left us technologically exposed. For a culture still coming of age in an era of connectivity, this marked an uncomfortable first.

As did most media outlets, KGO-TV covered the basics of Galaxy

4's failure. We explained the satellite's function, described the problem, and talked about solutions.

I began the story by visiting San Francisco's financial district. "How's your e-mail?" I pointedly asked one man.

"Smoke signals would work better right now," he said.

But, to me, Galaxy 4 also suggested a broader question about our newfound reliance on technology. On another level, was this about a broken satellite, or about us? It seemed to me that, until recently, the human race had managed just fine without wireless communication, and I had a small piece of local knowledge to help demonstrate it.

Fifteen years earlier, I'd purchased a mattress from the McRoskey Airflex Company. Recently, when that mattress wore out, I telephoned them to ask about a replacement. In a few seconds, the company's receptionist quoted what model I'd bought, the warranty, the date of purchase, and the price. "That's a fast computer," I remarked to her.

"We don't have computers." Nor, she added, did the company use e-mail, voicemail, printers, terminals, or pagers. Nothing. In ninety-nine years of business, the McRoskey Airflex Company never felt a need to modernize. Employees still filed paper receipts, used carbon copies, and alphabetized customer information on three-by-five cards.

When Galaxy 4 failed, I called McRoskey Airflex again and spoke with the same receptionist. "What does Galaxy 4 mean to you?"

"Nothing," she said.

That day, we rounded out the basic story by visiting the mattress company, with its fault-free, low-tech methods. While Galaxy 4 knocked the rest of us back to the 1960s, McRoskey Airflex had never left. In making the connection, we took the story a little deeper.

## What People Take Away: "The Lawn"

Sometime, somewhere, you must have played the telephone game. One person whispers in the ear of another, who then passes that message to the next person, who passes it again, and on down the line. It's not uncommon that, by the time the message goes full circle, it's taken on another meaning or context. This is a simple but effective example of how people look at or hear things and impart their own spin to them. They do it with paintings, music, plays, and television news stories.

So it shouldn't surprise you that no two viewers approach or interpret any one story the same way. They pick up shades and nuances, and build on them. Whereas one person might see a news story as a straightforward description of events, another might find humor in it. Sometimes this works to a reporter's detriment, and sometimes to his advantage.

In October 1999, our late and beloved assignment editor, Bill Magee, walked a press release over to my desk. He always had a sense of what his staff might like. "Hey, Wayno—I don't know if this is a story or not," he said. "It has that puff element, but you might find an angle." He was right.

That release came from a fertilizer company and announced the winners of a national lawn contest. Lo and behold, a second-place winner lived in our viewing area—one of ten. That's right. A woman from the East Coast finished first, and ten others finished second. To me, the company's math sounded like a blatant commercial ploy. Most reporters or assignment editors would see right through it, but I remembered a former neighbor who'd been a compulsive lawn addict. I played a hunch and made a call on the story.

The second-place winner's name was Ralph Gillibert, and his

lawn, in nearby Oakland, did not disappoint us. It measured twenty feet by twenty feet, and was green beyond all dreams. One could safely say that Ralph's lawn made artificial turf looked ragged by comparison, and, in just describing it, I still haven't done it justice.

The lawn was so grand, so magnificent, that it had become a neighborhood tourist attraction. When the neighbors had company, they routinely brought those guests for special viewings. Photographer John Griffin and I watched as one group of visitors stood piously in front of Ralph's meticulously painted fence. They peered, pointed, gawked, said, "Ooh," then, "Ahh," and snapped pictures.

You'd think they were visiting the Sistine Chapel of grass. Ralph certainly treated it that way. When he trimmed the edges, he would get down on his hands and knees, and use scissors. When he mowed, he did so based not on the day of the week or the time of day, but on the position of the sun.

Even Ralph's dog gave the lawn deferential treatment. The pooch never set a paw on it. Instead of walking across, he circled around.

Only Alice, Ralph's wife of thirty-four years, might not have been completely trained. Actually, it might have been the other way around. Early in their relationship, Alice recognized she'd married an obsessive perfectionist. "Dinner must be ready precisely at six," said Alice off-camera. "He wants us finished by six-thirty."

She recalled the occasion when Ralph yanked a dessert fork from her hand while she was still eating. "It was time to wash the dishes," she says he said.

Early in their marriage, Alice decided she could either fight Ralph's tendencies or deal with them, and that's where the lawn enters in. "It's a good place for him," Alice told us.

John Griffin and I quickly recognized that Alice Gillibert would play a big part in this story. We shot it as a give-and-take, moving between Alice in her kitchen and Ralph in his yard. Outside, he patiently explained the merits of mowing patterns at optimal blade settings of three-eighths of an inch. Inside, Alice showed wedding pictures and described the trials of life with Ralph. In terms of personality, the two of them were polar opposites—a perfect match, and they played off it. Thanks to the Gillibert's honesty and humor, we took an award-winning lawn and used it as the centerpiece of a character study:

### THE LAWN
### November 1999

[TRACK]
IF OUR LAWNS WERE CHILDREN, MOST OF US
WOULD BE DELINQUENT PARENTS.
OUR LAWNS ARE THE WAYWARD STUFF OF BEST
INTENTIONS, GONE TO SEED, OR AS RALPH
GILLIBERT WOULD SAY . . .

[SOT]
Ralph comments on other lawns: "Goat pasture."

[TRACK]
(we see Ralph on his hands and knees, edging his
lawn with a small scissors)

IF THOSE WHO LIVE IN GLASS HOUSES SHOULD NOT
THROW STONES, THIS IS A MAN WITH EVERY RIGHT
TO BE CRITICAL
HERE, IN A TWENTY-BY-TWENTY-FOOT SECTION IN
FRONT OF HIS OAKLAND HOME, RALPH SEEKS
NOTHING LESS THAN BLESSED PERFECTION.

[SOT]
Wayne: "ISN'T THIS SCISSOR BIT A LITTLE OVER-THE-
TOP?"

Ralph: "Quiet. I'm concentrating . . ."

[TRACK]
YOUR BARBER SHOULD BE AS METICULOUS.
YOUR MATE AS PATIENT.

[SOT]
Wayne asks Alice: "HE'S A PLANNER, AND YOU'RE A
. . . ?"

Alice: "Procrastinator."

[TRACK]
HE'S A NEAT FREAK. SHE'S . . .

[SOT]
Alice: "Loose."

[TRACK]
HE'S REGIMENTED. SHE'S . . .

[SOT]
Alice: "Casual."

[TRACK]
(we see their wedding picture)
RALPH AND ALICE ARE A CLASSIC EXAMPLE OF
OPPOSITES STILL ATTRACTING AFTER THIRTY-FOUR
YEARS.
HOW COULD SHE HAVE KNOWN THAT, WHEN SHE
MARRIED THE MAN, SHE WOULD SHARE HIM WITH A
LAWN . . .

[SOT]
Alice interrupts: "Every day. Every day he's working
on the lawn . . ."

[SOT]
Wayne to Ralph: "WHAT LENGTH OF BLADE DO YOU
USE?"

Ralph: "Three-eighths of an inch."

Wayne: "EXACTLY?"

Ralph: "Exactly."

[SOT]
(in the kitchen)
Wayne to Alice: "WHAT IF A NEIGHBOR COMES BY
WALKING HIS DOG, AND THE DOG GETS LOOSE?"

Alice: "Heeeh! That would be serious."

[TRACK]
IF LAWN CARE EVER BECOMES AN EXTREME SPORT,
RALPH WILL QUALIFY.
TO KEEP AN EYE ON IT, HE RARELY TAKES LONG
VACATIONS.
TO PROTECT IT DURING DROUGHTS, HE DUG A
WELL.
AND, WHEN FRIENDS VISIT NEIGHBORS, THEY BRING
THEM BY TO LOOK, BUT, AS WITH A FINE MUSEUM
PIECE, THEY ALSO KEEP A RESPECTFUL DISTANCE.

[SOT]
Alice points to the bricks that surround the lawn:
"Our own dog walks around the bricks . . ."

[TRACK]
(Wayne walks the bricks surrounding the lawn)
OR ANYONE. IF "POINT A" IS ON ONE SIDE . . . AND
"POINT B" ON THE OTHER, AN AVERAGE PERSON
WOULDN'T EVEN CONSIDER TAKING A DIRECT
ROUTE . . .

[STAND-UP]
(wide shot: Wayne stands on the bricks, looking at
the lawn)
TO DO SO WOULD SEEM . . . SACRILEGIOUS.

[SOT]
(we cut to a tight shot of Wayne's shoe: its toe
extends onto the grass; he quickly pulls it back)

[SOT]
Wayne to Ralph: "IF SOMEBODY WALKS ON THIS
LAWN IT BOTHERS, YOU, DOESN'T IT?"

Ralph: "Not really. Depends on who it is."

Wayne: "OK, LET'S SAY A SUMO WRESTLER WALKED
ON YOUR LAWN."

Ralph: "No, I wouldn't like that."

[TRACK]
BUT IF YOU LOOK AT IT, THERE'S A LITTLE OF
RALPH'S YARDENING OBSESSION IN EVERY ONE OF
US. WE ALL HAVE QUIRKS. MOST OF US WANT TO
DO AT LEAST ONE THING REALLY WELL . . .

[SOT]
Wayne to Ralph: "IS THERE REALLY SUCH A THING
AS A PERFECT LAWN?"

Ralph: "I don't believe so. I've never seen one."

[TRACK]
BUT HE'S CLOSER THAN HE THINKS BECAUSE,
SEVERAL MONTHS AGO, ALICE READ AN
ADVERTISEMENT FOR A NATIONAL LAWN
CONTEST . . .

[SOT]
Alice: "I took the pictures of it and filled out the
forms."

[TRACK]
AND RALPH WON. IT WAS NOTHING LESS THAN A
BENEDICTION. HE GOT A T-SHIRT AND 250 DOLLARS
CASH, AND BRAGGING RIGHTS BECAUSE NOW IT'S
OFFICIAL . . .
RALPH GILLIBERT'S LAWN FINISHED BEST IN THE
WEST.

[SOT]
As Ralph sits on his lawn, Wayne asks: "WAS THERE
A POINT IN YOUR LIFE WHEN YOU MIGHT HAVE
KNOWN YOU'D GONE OVER THE TOP WITH THIS?"

Ralph: "No." (laughs) "It just snuck up on me."

Wayne: "WELL, IT'S A BEAUTIFUL LAWN."

Ralph replies with dignity: "Thank you very much."

[TRACK]
AND MAYBE THAT'S WHAT HE REALLY WANTED.
NOTHING LIKE A COMPLIMENT TO KEEP A MAN
HAPPILY MOWING INTO THE SUNSET.

## Write Up to Your Viewers

Viewers still ask about that segment from time to time. It's satisfying because, when people criticize television news, they often say we make the mistake of telling them how to feel and what to take away from a story. But, when watching Ralph and Alice, viewers decide for themselves.

I've shown the piece to groups of people at least twenty times. After the story runs, I always ask what it was about. Answers range from obsession, to marriage, to patience, to the attraction of opposites. All are true.

No one, yet, has suggested that the story is about an immaculate lawn.

To me, that's a compliment.

# 19

## Finding Stories:
## Just Ask, Look, Listen, and Think

If you haven't heard of Fred Medill, someday you will. At fourteen years old, he had already become a force of nature.

Some kids play baseball with their fathers. Others go fishing. But Fred Medill and his father, Carey, gave a different kind of twist to father-son bonding. They hung with the paparazzi along Hollywood red carpets. "Maybe you could say we're fishing for a few celebs," suggested Carey.

The Medills' Tinseltown adventures began when Fred requested a star-studded home video for his bar mitzvah. His dad, a Beverly Hills attorney, helped Fred score interviews with Neil Sedaka, George Foreman, and Cameron Diaz. After her interview, in particular, the kid was hooked. He decided to become an entertainment reporter. From then on, two or three nights a week, after homework, Fred and Carey joined the rest of the Hollywood press watching stars, starlets, and wannabe stars and starlets wander past at movie premieres. Carey ran the camera. Fred asked the questions.

Give the youngster credit for being a fast learner. "They're just here to be seen and photographed," he said of the celebrities. "Some of them don't even know the name of the movie."

But they did know Fred, who was five feet, four inches tall and didn't even shave yet. He had a knack for leaning in, looking cute, stretching out his microphone, and getting the beautiful people to talk. Of Tom Cruise he once asked, "When you go on vacation, do you and Nicole take the kids with?"

Talk about chutzpah—in the ninth grade, Fred Medill notched an exclusive interview with President Bill Clinton at the ramp of Air Force One. "Do you think the new generation of American youth is more apathetic to the political fervor that existed in your time?"

"No," replied the president. Interview over. And Fred used it.

Once a week, he downloaded his interviews into a home computer and hosted his own webcast called *Fred TV*. What he lacked in ratings, Fred gained in experience.

In December 1999, KABC-TV photographer David Busse and I followed Fred around for a day. I remember asking this remarkable young man about what he'd learned from his adventures. "Just ask," said Fred, "because you never know what's going to come of it. Even if they say no, it never hurts. Just ask."

That's darn good advice for any journalist, whether he's fourteen and collecting movie stars, or forty and looking to do a segment for the evening news.

# They're On to Us

It's challenging for any reporter to find original, memorable stories five days a week. Anyone who pretends otherwise isn't telling the truth. Most reporters are naturally curious, but daily demands can make it difficult to see past the next deadline.

But it's important that we do take responsibility for at least some of our daily assignments. Our choices of stories define us as individuals, and as an industry. If we expect the viewers to respect us, we must also respect them. When you wonder why television news is losing audience shares, look at your coworkers, at your competitors across the street, and perhaps at yourself. If, as the critics say, television news caters to the lowest common denominator, it's partly because we've driven many of our viewers away. They're on to us. Every day, we cast the seeds of what may become our own irrelevance. Great numbers of viewers have stopped taking local television news seriously. They snicker at our self-importance. They're numb to any feigned immediacy. This shouldn't come as any big surprise. Chicken Little could shout, "The sky is falling," only so often before losing his credibility. The same can be said for us.

If all you knew of life came from local television news, you might think we live in a frightening, dangerous world. You might not want to risk going outside, even in daylight.

To serve our viewers, we need to do more stories about issues, politics, and that neighborhood around the corner. *Beyond being informative and relevant, television news must also be observational.* We should remember that most of our viewers live normal but interesting lives. When told well, stories about their relatively minor concerns, struggles, and victories can have universal appeal. It's the stuff of life.

# Find Your Own Stories

Finding good stories is the byproduct of listening, reading, and using your common sense. Look around. What are people talking about? What are they writing about?

When you get into a rhythm, story ideas begin to connect. One leads to another. While shooting a piece about teenage pilots, for instance, I had a casual conversation with a woman who had just purchased a ticket on a new, one-plane airline. That story, in turn, led to another about an eighty-year-old former stewardess.

## E-mails: Little Kabul

You'll find one good source of ideas in the letters and e-mails that viewers send to your station. Look through them occasionally. You may come across a news story.

During the war in Afghanistan, residents of Fremont, a suburban city south of San Francisco, wrote to complain about how the media referred to a small stretch of Afghan-owned storefronts and restaurants as "Little Kabul." "That section of town is in Fremont, and will always be Fremont," one woman wrote. "Why did the media change the name?"

We didn't. I made a couple of telephone calls and learned that those merchants gave the name Little Kabul to themselves. We simply repeated it. But those e-mails led to a segment that exposed the controversy, and explored how names or labels needlessly divide people.

## Newspapers: The "No-Swear" Lady

Every day, television news reporters adapt stories from newspapers. We tend to resent this, but no one orders us to follow a print story verbatim. Use the article, instead, as a starting place or tip sheet.

You can still do your own reporting. Newspaper items may suggest new angles or even better stories.

I recall reading one piece about minor league baseball in California's Central Valley. It made passing reference to a "no-swear lady" who attended games and chided players for saying dirty words. Whoever she was, she sounded like a character, so I did some research and found her in Visalia, California.

True to the article, Helen Luttrell sat behind the first base dugout at every Visalia Oaks home game. She always brought along a loud voice, a squirt bottle, a pail, and a brush. "The brush is for filthy language. When they swear, I tell 'em I'll wash their mouths out with soap like their grandmothers would do."

Can you imagine?

Helen's late husband had been a baseball fan, too. After he died, she continued attending every home game, but with renewed conviction, apparently.

"What exactly do you define as a filthy word?"

Helen fixed me with a stern look. "You know darn well what a filthy word is. I don't have to tell you," she lectured. It was absurd. Swearing comes to baseball players as casually as tobacco chewing, spitting, and crotch scratching. Helen Luttrell might as well have gone to a church and asked the preacher not to preach.

Our story took a strange left turn when Helen disclosed her feud with Rick Burleson, who managed a rival team. She made him out to be like the devil.

Two years earlier, when Burleson's squad gave up six runs in one inning, he made a few indelicate comments inside the dugout. From her seat above, Helen heard every detail. "If he used the f-word once, he used it twenty times," she said. "The way he yelled at his team made me want to cry. They're just boys."

Burleson, a grown man and ex–big leaguer, had little patience for

Helen's bucket, her soap, her brush, her opinions, or her mouth. He stepped from the dugout, stared up at her and said loudly, in front of everyone, "Ma'am, mind your own damn business."

What gall! Helen wrote an angry letter to the league, which forwarded it to Burleson, and that sealed their grudge. Whenever his team came to town, Burleson and Helen refused to make up.

"I walk to the other end of the dugout so I won't have to listen to her," said Burleson.

"You could make peace with him," I suggested to Helen.

"No, he's the one who should come to me and apologize."

Burleson wouldn't hear of reconciliation, either. I asked him, "If a man can't play baseball and say a dirty word or two, what good is the game?"

"I dunno," he said.

We presented the story as a major league feud in a minor league setting. "He won't even look at me," said Helen, with hurt in her eyes.

"Maybe if she brought me cookies, or something," suggested Burleson.

Not likely. But, from one line in a newspaper article, we found a human interest story with an ironic simple truth. Helen Luttrell simply wanted a small amount of attention, and a place in the game. But, when she stepped across the invisible line that separates fans from players, she went too far. In the words of Rick Burleson, she should have minded her own damn business.

# The Difference Between
# Identifying a Story and Finding One

Most reporters are inquisitive, but that doesn't mean all of them bring it to their work. They often separate personal interests from professional ones. They may see something and wonder about it, but never connect how, by asking a question, they might turn that curiosity into a story. They get too close to the material in their lives.

This has happened to me many times, but most memorably in my first year of marriage. Like other clueless newlywed males, I found myself needing to make apologies quite often, and did so with flowers from a small sidewalk stand along Union Street in San Francisco.

There, a hip young woman sold twenty-dollar bouquets while, four feet away, on the other side of a picture window, another woman worked in a real estate office, selling million-dollar homes. Four feet—they spent their days so close to each other that I always assumed they'd met.

They hadn't. One evening, during a casual conversation, the flower lady admitted she wasn't even sure of the real estate woman's name.

"Really?" That sounded odd, so I went inside and spoke with the real estate woman. She didn't know the flower lady's name, either.

"That's fascinating," I told her. "Don't change anything just because I asked, but would you mind if I bring a camera and do a story about the two of you sometime?"

"Maybe," she said. "Give a call if you want."

A week later, on a slow news day, photographer Pam Partee and I did a piece about their relationship, or the absence of it. The story had nothing to do with news and everything to do with a simple-truth theme—that, in a big city, the closer we are to someone, the more distance we need.

## STRANGERS
### July 1991

[SOT]
Cynthia, the real estate woman, on phone: "I'm
calling for Stephen Clark . . ."

[TRACK]
CYNTHIA CUMMINS IS INTENSE AND PROFESSIONAL.
SHE LIVES IN A WORLD OF BIDS, ESCROWS, AND
CLOSURES.
A BUSINESS LIFE OF APPOINTMENT BOOK
INCREMENTS.

[SOT]
Cynthia says: "Well, today my calendar is just
completely booked."

[SOT]
Outside we see Carol handing flowers to a customer:
"These are two dollars a stem. They came in this
morning and are really fresh . . ."

[TRACK]
CAROL GRAMADOS IS LIGHT AND BREEZY. HERS IS A
WORLD OF BUDS AND STEMS AND BLOOMS. A
BUSINESS LIFE BASED ON WHIMSY.

[SOT]
Carol says to customer: "And thank you . . ."

[TRACK]
THEY'RE TWO WOMEN, IN TWO DIFFERENT WORLDS,

SEPARATED BY JUST FOUR FEET AND A PANE OF
GLASS.

[SOT]
We pan from Carol outside to Cynthia, still talking
on the phone: "You haven't heard from her yet?"

[SOT]
Carol: "Sometimes we smile, once in a while."

Wayne: "ANYTHING ELSE?"

Carol: "No."

[SOT]
(inside the office)
Cynthia: "When I'm in here it's important that I
concentrate on what I'm doing. So I really have to
tune her out."

[STAND-UP]
(on the street)
IF YOU LOOK AROUND, YOU MAY FIND A CAROL OR
CYNTHIA IN ALL OUR LIVES. MAYBE WE PASS THEM
ON A HIGHWAY OR SHARE AN ELEVATOR WITH
THEM. MAYBE THEY EVEN LIVE RIGHT NEXT DOOR.
IT'S ALMOST AS IF THE CLOSER WE ARE TO
SOMEONE, THE MORE DISTANCE WE NEED.

[SOT]
Cynthia: "I think that's typical of life today. Most
people don't even have a pane of glass between
them. They're just sitting next to each other in an
office or on the bus. I mean, how much do any of us
know about each other?"

[TRACK]
CAROL AND CYNTHIA HAVE NEVER BEEN FORMALLY
INTRODUCED, EVEN THOUGH THEY'VE WORKED
WITHIN FOUR FEET OF EACH OTHER ABOUT TWO
YEARS NOW—ONE SELLING TEN-DOLLAR
BOUQUETS, AND THE OTHER, MILLION-DOLLAR
HOMES. THAT MUCH, WE KNOW.

[SOT]
Carol: "She's married. She works there. She's been
there a long time."

[SOT]
Cynthia: "Well I think she's a teenager. And she's
very sociable. She has a lot of friends who come by
. . ."

[SOT]
Carol: "She's into her work and I'm into mine. She's
really quiet and . . ."

[SOT]
Cynthia: " . . . Sometimes she plays her music a
little loud and I have to knock on the window and
motion to turn it down."

[TRACK]
NOW THE BIG QUESTION . . .

[SOT]
Wayne asks Carol: "DO YOU KNOW THE NAME OF
THE WOMAN IN THERE?"

Carol: "Cynthia."

[SOT]
Wayne asks Cynthia: "DO YOU KNOW THE NAME OF
THE WOMAN OUTSIDE?"

Cynthia: "No."

[TRACK]
CYNTHIA AND CAROL. SUCH FAMILIAR STRANGERS.
JUST AN OBSERVATION ABOUT LIFE IN THE BIG
CITY.

[SOT]
Wayne to Cynthia: "YOU DON'T KNOW WHERE SHE
LIVES OR ANYTHING ABOUT HER FAMILY?"

Cynthia: "No."

Wayne: "DO YOU WONDER?"

Cynthia: "I do now. But I think I better bone up."

## The Red House

My family lives on a ridge in San Anselmo, California. It's a nice house perched along environmental open space. We'd like to make it a different color, but City Hall won't let us. Our planning commission dictates the hues in which ridge dwellers may paint their homes. Only natural and bland will do.

We abide by the rules, however, so a few years ago my family and neighbors couldn't help but notice when, on an opposite ridge filled with equally bland homes, someone painted his house bright barn red. "It's a crimson eyesore," the neighbors said.

My daughter, Lauren, was three years old at the time. "Why did he do that, Daddy?"

"Because he's a goofball." We had a big laugh and, from then on, referred to the red house as "the Goofball House."

But Lauren had posed a good question—the most important one—"Why?" From that moment on we just had to know, so one afternoon we drove to the bottom of the red house's long driveway, left a note in the mailbox, and waited.

The next day, a man named Claude Reboul called. "Yes, I own the red house," he announced in a thick French accent.

"We were wondering why you painted it red."

"I cannot give you a straight answer. There is no such thing as a straight answer in life," said Claude.

A few days later, when photographer Charlie Jones and I visited him, Reboul proved it. Claude was a robust seventy-six years old, going on twenty-six, and anything but a goofball. The man simply loved life, and he insisted on popping a bottle of champagne to celebrate our meeting. "I live just outside the city lines," he explained. "I can paint my house any color. I can paint my house white. I can paint my house fluorescent green. I can paint my house orange-orange!"

But, as Claude explained, he'd painted it red in memory of his wife, Edith, with whom he'd spent forty-four years before her recent death. And his story was only beginning.

Claude Reboul grew up in France before World War II. When the Nazis invaded, he joined the underground movement. Before long, Claude dreamed of joining the Free French to fight the Germans in uniform, so he crossed the Pyrenees by foot. "It took twelve nights and thirteen days. I escaped from France and walked to Spain."

"You make it sound like a stroll through the park."

"Well, when you are sixteen years old, it is fun!"

Once in Spain, Claude surrendered to authorities, who put him in a prison he describes as more of a resort and a bureaucratic formality. The allies needed soldiers. Spain needed food. In return for one hundred pounds of flour, the Spanish traded Claude to the Free French, who sent him to Corpus Christi, Texas, for pilot training. Claude's first flight changed his life. "The instructor took me upside down, and I looked up, and there was a train above me!"

"You were hooked?"

"Completely."

The war ended before Claude could fire a shot. He made his way to New York, intending to take a ship home, but, just before leaving, he met Edith, who changed the course of his life, again. They married, and Claude Reboul stayed in the United States.

"But why red?"

"Her favorite color," said Claude as we walked around outside. "Red is the color of joy and happiness. Look at the gold of the hills. Look at the blue sky. Look how beautiful it is. Red!"

It seemed we'd found our answer, but the day still held one more surprise. Every Sunday afternoon my wife and daughter and I would notice an airplane buzzing the ridge around Claude's house. We always wondered about it, and, after Claude told his story, I remembered the plane.

"Is that you, Claude?"

"Well, of course!"

"That's the other reason?"

"So I can see my house!"

*We asked a question, and found a story.* Claude Reboul taught us a lesson about how one turn in life leads to another, and how men become the sum of their experiences.

A teenager.

A war.

A lifetime adventure.

A red house on a hill.

# 20

---

## One Story, Start to Finish

---

High-wire acrobats and television news reporters have plenty in common. Acrobats take risks every time they go to work. Reporters take risks every time they push a deadline.

Acrobats cannot effectively function without confidence.

Neither can reporters.

If an acrobat slips or loses his balance, he instinctively knows where to catch the wire and save himself. When a reporter slips while working a story, he "catches the wire," too, but in an editorial way.

For both the acrobat and the reporter, failure is not an option.

# New York City

That describes my predicament in New York City during the fall of 2001. A month after the September 11 attacks, KGO-TV photographer Michael Clark and I had just crossed the nation by train. In a time when terrorist threats and anthrax scares dominated the news, we picked towns at random, left the train and shot nine small stories, each a reflection of the much bigger one. Did the attacks change people? Could normal life still exist? Had the experience pushed Americans further apart, or brought them closer together? Later, "Stories from the Heartland," as we called it, became a half-hour program.

In keeping with the trip's character, Mike and I hadn't made plans for our piece in New York City. We would visit Ground Zero and see what we could find. Just one problem. New York City is more complicated than, say, Mount Pleasant, Iowa. We didn't know the local geography. I had no name or face recognition, nor the home-field connections for gaining access.

But Mike and I did have an expense account, so we ditched the rental car and hired a limousine. That sounds extravagant, but follow my logic. The limo would cost less than keeping a taxi all day. The driver would be working for us. He'd know his way around town, we wouldn't have to find parking, and we could use his trunk to store equipment. Should we need to move quickly or get more gear, the car could come to us.

Here, then, is what happened as we searched for a story at Ground Zero. The experience reinforces many lessons in this book, from characterization, to interviewing, to following spontaneous leads, to reporting what you find, to writing, structure, and simple truths. Later, when reading the script, you'll see how the piece came together.

## Police State

The car met us at ten in the morning and delivered us into heavy financial-district congestion about one hour later. With every passing block, the neighborhood surrounding Ground Zero looked more like a police state. Howard Price, the assignment manager at our sister station, WABC-TV, had said to expect as much: "There's plenty of security, but it leaks like a sieve."

Police and military types guarded every intersection. They scrutinized buses, trucks, and people. We carried San Francisco and California press credentials, but nothing official from New York City. Mike and I gambled that we could walk and talk our way in.

"We're from ABC in San Francisco," Mike or I would tell police.

"Where's your identification?" they would ask.

"Sir, we've traveled across the country by train, stopped in small towns along the way, and now we have one day left in New York. We can spend it in bureaucracy or we can try to find a story. Do we look like terrorists?"

This worked, several times.

Ten blocks from Ground Zero, our car could approach no closer, so we exchanged wireless phone numbers with the driver, left him to orbit the area, and set out on foot.

## Possible Stories Everywhere

When beginning this kind of shoot, whatever you see has story potential because you don't yet know what your focus will be. You don't have a main character. You may not even have an angle. At best, you have a wirewalker's confidence that you'll develop something. "See what you can find" stories move you around like waves or gusts of wind. Catch them; ride them; see where they take you. Trust your curiosity.

We walked two blocks and saw a basketball court. Outside, on the chainlink fence, inspectors had attached a note declaring the area free from asbestos contamination. That seemed a bit odd, so Michael took pictures. Inside, a racially mixed group of young men played a full-court game. Strange—ten blocks from a mass grave, they could turn their backs on tragedy and play hoops. Why?

"We've got to move on with our lives," explained Anthony Torres while waiting for the next game. "We can't stay depressed."

A second kid, Demetrius Padmore, joined in. "If we sit here and mourn, they get the best of us, you know?"

Both comments made good sound bites. I hoped they might say even more, and tried to push the first kid, Anthony, to the next level. "Let's say you got Osama bin Laden in a room, just you and him, one-on-one . . ."

Anthony cleared his throat and stammered. His gentle face turned hard and mean. He paused, and then said with resolve, "I'd end him."

## A Look Inside

We walked on, following Ground Zero's fenced-off, guarded perimeter. To a casual eye, the place looked more like a construction zone than the scene of a terrorist attack. Inside, cranes performed a repetitive ballet against a backdrop of ripped, torn, and gutted buildings. We saw the Stars and Stripes everywhere—on hats, clothing, and façades.

"Is there a better vantage point for looking inside?" I asked a policeman.

"That way," he pointed. "Keep going." We did, following makeshift barricades that seemed to stretch for miles.

By now, you've certainly seen pictures of Ground Zero's destruction, but they don't do justice to the width, the depth, or the tickling sensation from a fine dust coating the backs of our throats. September 11 turned the neighborhood into a ghost city of eerily empty skyscrapers with chained and padlocked revolving doors.

Photographically, Michael couldn't miss.

We spotted some civilian types. The WABC-TV assignment manager had said, "It's become a tourist attraction," but this wasn't like any other tourist attraction you've ever visited. It didn't have the slightest hint of commercialism. No one hawked souvenirs. No one acted loud, rude, or disrespectful. Those "tourists" would peer through a fence or around a corner. They'd shake their heads and then solemnly walk away.

We approached several who didn't care to talk, but Rose and Bob Lamano, from Bedford, Virginia, kindly gave us a few minutes. "I grew up in New York," she said. "I never expected such a large area. To me, it's a little like stepping on holy land. I just felt like I wanted to be here."

Bob finished for her. "Initially, I didn't want to come here at all. It was like an invasion of privacy for those who died, but it's something we wanted to see to make us stronger. I just feel for all the people who lost loved ones, is all I can say."

As the Lamanos wandered away for one last look, Mike and I hiked along the Hudson River and rounded a corner roughly one hundred yards from what used to be the World Trade Center's atrium. Above and beyond, we stared at a gap in the sky where, before September 11, the Twin Towers had stood.

"Hard to believe they used to be there," I remarked to Michael.

The skyline looked like a familiar, friendly face, but one with the teeth knocked out.

"Yep," he said.

## Let the Story Find You

Often as not, you'll find your story line in this kind of piece by letting it find you. Thus far, we'd come across useful material, but nothing exceptional. Then we noticed a disheveled, frenetic woman taking pictures of the gap between the buildings. "They were there?" I asked in confirmation.

"Behind that last arch." She pointed. "To the south of that crane was a tower. No hole. No hole. No death."

Her name was Deborah Ortega. She used to live in the neighborhood and said she still considered Ground Zero as home. "Were you here on September 11?" I asked.

Deborah pulled a photo album from under her arm and turned page after page of pictures showing the skyscrapers burning. "This is what we saw from the window," she said, pointing to a photo of the second tower. "I show these to people and tell them that this is my home, and this is my view, and then they kind of get it."

Deborah Ortega needed people to understand what she and her neighbors survived, and continued to endure. She spoke of the destroyed World Trade Center the way others might describe a divorce or a dead family member. "I try to come back as much as I can just to get used to the idea of this place as it is now."

"Sounds like you have a lot of baggage . . ."

"Big baggage," she nodded through blinking, tear-reddened eyes. Deborah had a lost look on her face. It froze me. I had nothing to say. As happens so often, she took that as a cue to open up. "I saw about twenty people fall from those towers, and I felt like such a coward as I rode my bike away and knew I couldn't help them. But then I felt so bad for them up there. You could see them at the windows and see them wanting to get out. And we knew this was not a Bruce Willis movie where everything ends so happily, you know?"

Later, her description timed out to twenty-three seconds, but it was so chilling that we used every word. Deborah Ortega would be worth following. "What else are you doing today?" I asked.

"Helping a friend move."

"From where?"

"Up there." Deborah pointed to an apartment tower across the street. "She lives on the thirty-second floor. You can see everything from there."

And so our piece began to take shape. In Deborah Ortega we found both a good character and an insider who could take us deeper into Ground Zero than any press credential. "Will your friend talk to us?" I asked.

"I'll call." Deborah dug a telephone from her purse and handed it over. After a few minutes of gentle persuasion her friend, Anita Glesta, invited us up.

"This way." Deborah hurried us along, never pausing or even looking as we came upon a mountain of teddy bears, flowers, and photographs. Emotionally, it stopped us cold. The memorial must have been shoulder high and seventy-five feet long. Those teddy bears, piled on top of each other, might as well have been bodies. In a visual way, Mike and I then understood how many people died there on September 11. You cannot imagine a more sad, sobering tribute.

But Deborah didn't want to dwell there. She didn't even want to look. "We have to go now," she said. "Anita's almost finished with the movers."

Mike and I thought about staying to shoot a sequence, but in doing so we would have lost Deborah. Besides, we could return later. Deborah led us past a barricade, through a courtyard then a building, and finally into an elevator. As the door closed, a man tried to force his way in with us. "Who the hell are you? You're not allowed in this building!" he shouted.

I felt protective of Deborah Ortega, and our story. "We're the news. And who the hell are you?" Deborah explained he was the assistant building manager. He had ignored her for a month, until that moment.

"You'll have to leave," the assistant manager said. "You need written permission before entering the building."

I didn't buy it. "You don't know the law, do you? You're way out of line. Now smile for the camera." He backed off as the elevator door closed.

## A Second Main Character

Deborah's friend, Anita Glesta, is an artist and single mother. As we entered her apartment, the movers were taking the last of her furnishings and sculpture. We'd planned only to use her window for an overview of Ground Zero, but, after one look at her frown-frozen face, we knew she had plenty to say.

Michael went to the window for his shot looking down into the ruins. Then Anita showed us around her empty apartment, explaining where the furniture used to be and how it had fit. On the kitchen doorjamb, we traced the growth spurts of her twin twelve-year-old boys.

"This was the living room, this was the kitchen, and this is where the boys slept."

"Quite a view," I observed. "And I'll bet you paid a lot for it."

"We paid New York City prices. It is still impossible for me to look at the view now. And to think of moving back is inconceivable."

I asked the inevitable, obvious question, "Were you here?"

"Yes, I saw everything," Anita said stoically. "I heard the noise and saw the tail of the plane disappear into the building. Then I saw fire and knew immediately that we were in big trouble." Anita described stuffing her passport and telephone into a purse and running to the elevator. "About halfway down, the whole building started vibrating and then the door opened." She told how she took stairs the rest of the way, emerging just after the second plane hit. "When I got to ground level I kept running. I was struck by how everyone was just standing there in shock. They stood in utter disbelief, just watching this."

Michael and I moved Anita to a second angle and asked more questions. I suggested that, if one could come up with a physical description of her mental state, it would be "battered and bruised—emotionally black-and-blue."

"Scarred," she corrected me.

"Will you ever get over this?"

"I don't know yet. I don't know," said Anita, almost wistfully.

It was enough. We thanked both Anita and Deborah for trusting us with their stories. Before meeting them, Michael and I hadn't thought of Ground Zero as a neighborhood. After, we looked at the entire country that way.

"We're victims, too," Anita added as we left. "We're victims of a crime, but we're not getting any help. The Red Cross won't give us anything without receipts, and, at best, then we get bread crumbs." Michael picked up the camera again as Anita spent five minutes venting against the government. "There has been no emotional— no umbrella support either financially or emotionally for people who lived at Ground Zero. It's outrageous and shocking."

One hour earlier, we hadn't had a story. An hour later, we'd found too much of one. I was still trying to figure how to include

Anita's closing tirade when Michael's camera began misbehaving. To fix it, he would have to walk down and meet the car, roughly a forty-minute round trip. He'd never get past the assistant manager again. That simplified our decision.

I left with Michael and waited at the teddy bear memorial, watching a cross-section of Americans wander past: civil servants, executives, blue collar people, men and women in uniform. They looked at the pictures, read the tributes, and got misty-eyed. Most of the men didn't come back. But the women would move close, take a long look, build up a torrent of tears, walk away, and then re-turn, as if to fill up with grief to purge again.

When Michael came back he spent twenty minutes shooting the teddy bears, the visitors, and their reactions. He simply set the cam-era on his tripod and let the action work through the frame. Then I asked a few people if their residual emotions surprised them. "I had that week of sorrow," confided one woman. "But coming here brought it back."

"Had you thought you were over the pain?" I asked another.

"When I came here, I thought I was over this, but not at all." She began to cry.

Finally, and mostly because KGO-TV had sent us across the country to New York City, we shot a stand-up. I felt weird doing it, and didn't think we would use it:

> [STAND-UP]
> AND YET THERE IS MORE HERE THAN THE OBVIOUS
> GRIEF . . . MORE THAN THE FACT THAT THIS IS A
> WAR ZONE AND ALSO A CRIME SCENE, BECAUSE, IF
> YOU LOOK ABOVE, YOU'LL SEE APARTMENT
> BUILDINGS. PEOPLE FORGET THAT GROUND ZERO IS
> ALSO A NEIGHBORHOOD.

## Too Much Story?

Three hours after getting to Ground Zero without knowing what we would find, a strong story had, instead, found us. The challenge would be in writing it.

I did have time on my side, and probably too much. The segment would air two weeks later as the conclusion of our series. Two weeks to analyze and overthink it. Two weeks to describe three hours in three minutes. Three minutes is a long time in television news, but not when trying to combine the following elements:

1. The kids playing basketball
2. The sense of Ground Zero being a police state
3. Pictures of the demolition zone
4. Pictures of the hole in the ground
5. The tourists
6. The teddy bear memorial
7. People reacting to the teddy bears
8. Two main characters, Deborah and Anita
9. The concepts of Ground Zero as a neighborhood, and how what happened there unified the nation

Three minutes.

## Writing Block

On Thanksgiving Day 2001, I sat down at my desk in San Francisco to write the story. How would it begin? My head told me to start with teddy bears because they were the strongest element, but then what?

In the first draft, I aimed for something dramatic:

> [TRACK]
> NEW YORK HAS BECOME A CITY OF HOLES. THERE

IS ONE IN THE SKY, ANOTHER IN THE GROUND,
AND, AT WHAT USED TO BE THE WORLD TRADE
CENTER, THERE IS THE BIGGEST HOLE—IN ITS
HEART.

That had potential, but it didn't lead anywhere. It established a mood, but might confuse the timeline. After a cup of coffee and a walk around the building, I tried a different open:

[TRACK]
NEW YORK CITY'S NEWEST TOURIST ATTRACTION HAS
A PERFECT VIEW OF THE STATUE OF LIBERTY, BUT
NOT THE SLIGHTEST HINT OF COMMERCIALISM . . .

I worked with that for a while, added a couple of sound bites, drank another cup of coffee, looked at the copy again, and hated it. I was trying to write to a formula, but the experience defied one. This piece needed understatement.

After a third cup of coffee, a concept took shape. Every install-ment in this series had been a travelogue, eschewing more fancy techniques in favor of linear progressions. Why stop now? It goes back to the theory of writing what you find. I would tell the story of our day at Ground Zero as it happened.

Isn't that strange? After two weeks of internal debate, I began the story at the beginning. Having committed, the script practically wrote itself in about half an hour:

## GROUND ZERO
### From "Stories from the Heartland"
### November 2001

[TRACK]
(we see a basketball game)
IF YOU LISTEN TO THE PUBLIC RELATIONS PEOPLE,

NEW YORK CITY IS GETTING BACK TO NORMAL.
AND, TEN BLOCKS FROM GROUND ZERO, A PERSON
MIGHT ALMOST BELIEVE IT . . .
BUT ASK A POINTED QUESTION . . .

[SOT]
Wayne to Anthony Torres: "LET'S SAY YOU GOT
OSAMA BIN LADEN IN A ROOM, JUST YOU AND
HIM, ONE ON ONE . . ."

Anthony: "I'd end him."

[TRACK]
FOR TWO WEEKS, WE HAD TRAVELED EAST BY
TRAIN, AND THE CLOSER WE CAME TO NEW YORK
CITY, THE STRONGER THE PULL OF WHAT HAPPENED
HERE.
GROUND ZERO IS NOW, EFFECTIVELY, A POLICE
STATE . . . AN OTHER-WORLDLY NO-MAN'S LAND
THAT HAS ALSO BECOME A TOURIST ATTRACTION—
BUT THERE'S NOTHING COMMERCIAL ABOUT IT.

[SOT]
Bob Lamano: "Initially, I didn't want to come here at
all. It was like an invasion of privacy for those who
died, but it's something we wanted to see to make
us stronger. I just feel for all the people who lost
loved ones, is all I can say."

[TRACK]
(we cut to pictures of people grieving by the teddy
bear memorial)
NOTHING YOU HAVE READ OR SEEN CAN PREPARE
YOU.

NOTHING WARNS YOU ABOUT ROUNDING A CORNER
AND SEEING A MOUNTAIN OF TEDDY BEARS . . .
TO THIS DAY, GROUND ZERO REMAINS A
GRAVEYARD WHERE THOUSANDS DIED. FOR NOW,
THESE ARE ITS INNOCENT, FUZZY TOMBSTONES.

[SOT]
One of the women: "When I came here, I thought I
was over this, but not at all . . ."

[TRACK]
EVERY DAY, WORKMEN CARRY AWAY MORE OF THE
PHYSICAL DEBRIS, BUT THE EMOTIONAL KIND
REMAINS. IMAGINE LIVING HERE AND WATCHING
THE ATTACK HAPPEN.

[SOT]
Deborah Ortega points to the wreckage: "Behind that
last arch. To the south of that crane was a tower. No
hole. No hole. No death."

[TRACK]
IT SPEAKS VOLUMES ABOUT DEBORAH ORTEGA THAT,
AS SHE WALKS AROUND TOWN, SHE CARRIES A
SCRAPBOOK WITH PICTURES FROM HER APARTMENT.

[SOT]
Deborah: "I saw about twenty people fall from those
towers, and I felt like such a coward as I rode my
bike away and knew I couldn't help them. But then I
felt so bad for them up there. You could see them at
the windows and see them wanting to get out. And
we knew this was not a Bruce Willis movie where
everything ends so happily, you know?"

[TRACK]
EVEN TODAY, PEOPLE TRY TO GET AWAY.
DEBORAH TOOK US TO A NEIGHBOR'S PLACE, ANITA
GLESTA . . . FINALLY MOVING FROM AN APARTMENT
VIEW SHE CAN'T BRING HERSELF TO LOOK AT.

[SOT]
Wayne: "YOU SAW IT HAPPEN?"

Anita: "I saw everything. I heard the noise and saw
the tail of the plane disappear into the building.
Then I saw fire and knew immediately that we were
in big trouble."

[TRACK]
WE ALL KNEW . . . WE ALL SAW, AND THAT
TROUBLE SPREAD ACROSS THIS LAND.
MAYBE, UNTIL NOW, YOU NEVER THOUGHT OF
GROUND ZERO AS A NEIGHBORHOOD, BUT IT IS.
AND MAYBE, UNTIL NOW, YOU NEVER THOUGHT OF
AMERICA AS BEING PART OF THAT NEIGHBORHOOD,
BUT, EMOTIONALLY, WE ARE.
WHAT HAPPENED HERE EXTENDS TO EACH OF US.

[SOT]
Wayne to Anita: "IF ONE WERE TO DESCRIBE YOUR
EMOTIONAL CONDITION IN A PHYSICAL STATE, IT
MIGHT BE BATTERED AND BRUISED—EMOTIONALLY
BLACK-AND-BLUE."

Anita: "Scarred."

[TRACK]
IF YOU COME TO NEW YORK CITY, GROUND ZERO IS
SOMETHING TO VISIT, TO MOURN, AND THEN PUT
SOMEWHERE SAFE.

IF YOU LIVE HERE, IT'S A HOLE IN THE SKY . . .
ANOTHER IN THE GROUND . . . AND A BIG ONE IN
THE HEART.

[SOT]
Wayne to Anita: "WILL YOU EVER GET OVER THIS?"

Anita: "I don't know yet. I don't know."

[TRACK]
WE WILL. IT JUST TAKES TIME.

## Post Script

After the story aired, my daughter, who was then seven years old, asked about it at bedtime. "Daddy, who were all those teddy bears?"

"Moms and dads, son and daughters, brothers, sisters, aunts, uncles, neighbors, friends and friends of friends," I answered.

In retrospect, that might have made a nice line. Then again, it wasn't necessary.

# 21

## Change the Small Worlds First

Many people enter journalism and television news with the notion of changing the world, but, in fact, most of us of us will hardly nudge it. Instead, the world we cover is more likely to change us.

Take heart, however. There is a difference between the world as a whole, and the countless small worlds of individual men and women. Those are where, as a television news reporter, you can make a difference. If, in your work, you inform, enlighten, or influence one person, or if you do a story that touches someone's life for the better, then you can change personal worlds every day.

With that in mind, treat every story, and accordingly every world, with care and respect.

Take them one at a time.

# The One Book Bookstore

I can think of no better example than a segment I did for CBS News about Walter and Deloris Swan. For most of their years, the couple lived a quiet, honest life of obscurity in Bisbee, Arizona, a small tourist town just north of the Mexican border. Then, in old age and much to their surprise, Walter and Deloris became the main characters in a sweet and inspiring story.

Bisbee is a long way from anywhere else. To get there, photographer Dave Dellaria and I flew into Tucson, drove out past a graveyard for old airplanes near the airport, and headed south across the great emptiness. Nothing compares with an arid, dusty desert sunset when your only contact with civilization is a rental car, a black ribbon of striped asphalt, and a quart of bottled water.

Walter, in his eighties, had worked his entire life in Bisbee, as a plasterer. He and Deloris spent more than fifty married years together, and raised nine children.

"Money was always tight," Walter told us. The family didn't have color television or videos or much for entertainment. But Walter made up for it by coaxing the kids into bed each night with true stories of growing up in Bisbee with his brother, Henry. Walter would tell the kids of the first time he saw an airplane, or how a goat ate his schoolbooks, or about his first pair of shoes.

The children particularly enjoyed his story about the polliwogs. Walter would describe how, after big rains in the summer, he and his friends would visit a nearby "puddle hole," as he called it, to cool off in the water. One day, they found the puddle hole filled with blue-belly polliwogs. Water and Henry took the critters home as pets and left them in a big water bucket on the kitchen counter.

No one thought of the polliwogs again until the middle of that night, when Walter's father got up thirsty. He stumbled to the kitchen, fumbled around in the dark, and found a glass. "Then," said Walter, "I was woke by somebody coughing and gagging in the other room. I had the funniest feeling in the pit of my stomach. I knew just what had happened."

Sure enough, Walter's father had dipped his glass into the polliwog bucket instead of the drinking water, and taken a big gulp.

Now imagine a childhood of such bedtime stories from Walter, who was an artist with the spoken word.

Years later, after the kids moved out, when Walter and Deloris had only themselves and not much to do, she made a suggestion. "Walter, you should take those bedtime stories and write a book."

"But I can't write," he replied, and it was true. During our visit Walter pulled out his childhood report cards as proof. Sure enough, he made a string of Ds in composition.

Walter Swan might have been a bad English student, but, as a natural storyteller, he innately knew the rules of structure better than almost anyone, so he rose to the challenge and spent nights at the kitchen table, writing the tales in longhand. Deloris deciphered his chicken scratches, corrected them, and entered his work into a computer.

When they finished, the couple sent copies of their manuscript, called *Me 'n Henry*, to fourteen publishers. In return, they received fourteen rejections.

Many authors would have given up at that, especially if they'd spent most of their lives in an old mining town thousands of miles from those lofty New York publishing houses. "Still, we had faith in it," Deloris said. They were naïve, but the couple had courage, too. Walter and Deloris believed in *Me 'n Henry* so much that they used most of their life savings to publish a few hundred copies.

"The first time I held that book, I got all choked up," said Walter, who fought tears again in describing the moment.

He and Deloris made a novel plan. They took their book to the Arizona State Fair, set up a booth, and began doing business.

*Me 'n Henry* sold out.

Encouraged, the couple printed more.

This time, they rented space on Bisbee's main drag and opened a small storefront called the One Book Bookstore. On the shelves, piled high, they placed thousands of copies of *Me 'n Henry.* Walter's book was the store's only commodity and, as at the state fair, it sold.

Tourists would wander in. Walter, with his long gray hair, smiling face, and faded blue overalls, would spin a yarn or two, charm them, and then ask innocently, "Would you like to buy a book?" Who could say no? Walter Swan, the author, personally autographed every copy, for which he and Deloris received twenty dollars.

"It was more money than we'd ever seen before in all our lives," Deloris said.

We asked what difference the money had made for them. "Oh, I can go to the grocery store now and buy anything I want," Deloris told us. "No more counting pennies. We can afford anything."

And what was her favorite indulgence?

"I just love that artificial crab," Deloris confessed.

It was a funny line, but we never used it because she hadn't meant it that way. After this late financial success in their lives, the Swans finally had enough money to import real crab if they wanted, but their worldliness hadn't yet caught up to their finances. Why make a point of it and possibly embarrass them?

The Swans were about optimism, perseverance, and success. We can learn plenty from their story, particularly those of us who work in television news. When you believe in yourself, act on it, work at it, and never give up, good stuff happens.

## The Most Important Lesson

Sometimes reporters receive their most profound satisfactions from the simplest pieces. Walter Swan's bookstore was one of them. Our story didn't make much difference to the Swans at that point. Walter and Deloris could have taken or left being on the network news. After all they'd been through, it was gravy on top of a wonderful life together, and little more.

But, the night after our piece aired on *CBS This Morning,* I stayed up late and tuned in David Letterman. Either he or someone on his staff had seen our segment. And who did Letterman fly to New York City to be his guest?

It was Walter Swan telling bedtime stories again, not just to his kids this time, but to the biggest audience of them all, America.

He looked like the happiest man on Earth.

It made me happy, too. Sometimes the most profound rewards in this work come not from making big splashes, but from sitting back and watching what happens when the ripples lap onto shore.

# Acknowledgments

It's humbling to realize that most of what I know about packaging television news can be told in fewer than sixty thousand words. After twenty-five years of work, that's all—not even one full floppy disk.

Writing a book is like someone asking if you can swim twenty miles. You figure a mile a day . . . anybody can work up to that. But you don't anticipate winds, storms, fog, or currents. In the end it's much more than twenty miles. You reach mid-channel and then realize how, having gotten there, only you can swim in and finish it off.

Thanks to my wife, Susan, for encouraging me to write this book, and for naming it at the dinner table one night. Neither of us anticipated how much time and attention the manuscript would take. Susan, you got the short end of this deal. You already knew you married an obsessive man, but this book forced you to new levels of sainthood.

I thank my daughter, Lauren, for going to bed on time (mostly), which allowed me to get to the computer on time. After a few months of writing, she mounted a toy plastic horse atop the monitor. From then on, she referred to this project as "Daddy's brain-sucking horse." Lauren, thanks for sitting in the office and keeping me company on those early weekend mornings.

Thanks to my parents, Mike and Alicia Freedman. Parents are unconditional fans. Kids need them, even when they're all grown up. Dad, I wish you were still here to hold this book in your hands.

For his practical help, my deepest thanks go to Mervin Block, who put a bug in the ear of the publisher and made this book happen. That took faith, and also courage after Merv saw some early chapters. Merv, you showed me what it takes to write a book. You challenged me to seek a higher standard. You influenced my work in broadcasting. At forty-nine years old, it's nice to find a mentor.

Thanks to my editor, Devon Freeny, who never complained about my multitude of small changes. Devon, you made the right suggestions in just the right places, and kept me positive. You're a patient man.

Finally, thanks to KGO-TV photographer Michael Clark, who won't have to read this book because he's already heard it, over and over, through blizzards, floods, fires, baseball playoffs, cross-country train trips, and on, and on, and on.

As for the people below, thanks for listening, thanks for looking, and, in many cases, thanks for saying less instead of more. To some of you, thanks for showing me right from wrong in television news. To others, thanks for having faith and putting yourselves on the line for me. Most of you share something in common. You learned through experience to never again ask Wayne Freedman, "How's the book?"

To answer the question, it's finished.

| | | |
|---|---|---|
| Joe Ahern | Ron Brown | Mike Ferring |
| Jaie Avila | Cathy Cavey | Craig Franklin |
| Herb Bennett | Krisann Chasarik | Tom Fox |
| John Blackstone | Lucille Clark | Lynn Friedman |
| Scott Buer | Michael Clark | Ron Guintini |
| David R. Busse | CoCo | George Griswold |
| Charles Brown | Randy Davis | Todd Hanks |
| Karen Brown | Herb Dudnick | Steve Hartman |

| | | |
|---|---|---|
| Heather Ishimaru | Karen O'Leary | Valari Staab |
| Carolyn Johnson | John Odell | Randy Steinman |
| Kevin Keeshan | Dr. Robert Papper | Rick Swanson |
| Don Knapp | Lloyd Patterson | Ken Swartz |
| Leonard Koppett | Phyllis Pecorak | James Sudweeks |
| Doug Laughlin | Larry Pond | Eric Thomas |
| Adrienne Laurent | Rosendo Pena | Tim Tison |
| Art Linkletter | Dave Pera | Al Tompkins |
| Steve Lentz | Ike Pigott | Elsa Trexler |
| Devorah Major | Lou Prato | John Turner |
| Kerry McGee | Stephanie Riggs | Bobby Vermiglio |
| Bill McKnight | Karina Rusk | Lori Webster |
| Mackie Morris | John Sheehan | Milt Weiss |
| Dick Nelson | Andrew Shinnick | Catherine Welch |

# Index

ABC-TV (Los Angeles), 24
ad-libbing, 159–60, 161–63, 168–69
AIDS epidemic, 203
Allen, Gleena, 120–21
anchors, 66, 174–76
animals as subjects, 30–35, 215, 228–29
antimisting kerosene, 66–68
apartment hunter, 22–30
Armstrong, Neil, 221
Artavia, Joey, 74–76
Arthur, Scott, 157
*Art Linkletter's House Party* (CBS), 55–56
audience interest development. *see* interview techniques; story development techniques
auto accident with boy's shoe, 40
auto theft ring, 233–36
Avila, Jaie, 71

B-24 bomber, 170–71
background noise, 44, 213
background visuals, 123, 170–71, 172
Baldwin, Steve, 191, 193
Barantschik, Alexander, 79–80
baseball and swearing rights, 250–52
"Benihana trap," 200
Bisbee, Ariz., 278–80
black humor, 179–86
Blackstone, John, 173–74

Block, Mervin, 209
Borba, Rick, 132–33
Brennan, Robert "Rubidub," 112–15
Bronstein, Phil "Mr. Sharon Stone," 69–70
Brown, Charles, 57–61
bubble gum test, 88–89
Buchanan, Edna, 119
Burleson, Rick, 251–52
Bushard, Norman, 112–15
Busse, David, 70–71, 248
Bybee, Loren and Maureen, 224, 229–30

cable-car bell-ringing championships, 71–72
Caldwell, Doug, 111
California unemployment rate, 16–22
"Cal Ripkin's Last Game in Oakland," 103–6
cameras, 45, 92, 124–25, 156, 161–63, 170
Candlestick Park and Macy's, 201–3
careers. *see* television news reporting as a career
Carvers, Nev., 158
Catholics in San Francisco, 200–203
cat on power pole, 215
Cattrell, Joey, 14–15
Cavey, Cathy, 124–25, 158, 161
CBS News, 173, 218

*CBS This Morning,* 281

challenges. *see* television news crew
   challenges

Chambers, Ariz., 72–74, 78

chameleon theory, 17–18

character studies, 238–45, 250–52,
   252–59, 257–59

children
   first grader's first day, 89–90
   14-year-old entertainment reporter,
      247–48
   girl with the red ball, 54
   interviewing, 54–57, 90
   rookie baseball league, 222

chroma-key, 156

CID (Controlled Impact
   Demonstration), 66–68

"Claire the Goldfish," 31–35

Clark, Michael, 222, 262–70

clemency hearing for convicted
   murderer, 173

clichés, 169, 206

Clinton, Bill, 106–9, 248

"Clinton in the Woods," 108–9

closings
   examples, 16, 74, 121, 169, 221, 222
   humorous, 80, 230–31, 245
   live shot inserts, 172–73
   overview, 77–78
   sentiment in, 76, 78–80
   sound bites for, 77, 172
   tags, 170–71, 172
   with a twist, 80–82
   *see also* openings

"c'mon," use of, 48

CNN, 174

Community Rentals, 23–24

comparisons, using, 139–49

contrasts, using, 139–49

convicted murderer's clemency
   hearing, 173

Corolla and Nova as one, 90–91

*The Corpse Had a Familiar Face*
   (Buchanan), 119

Costner, Kevin, 159–60

counterpoint, 139–49

"Crash, Bang, 'Go Raiders!'" 134–37

Cruise, Tom, 248

Cummins, Cynthia, 254–59

daily news stories, 14, 22, 39

D'Aria, Lou, 217

Darwinism in news reporting, 93–94

data maintenance, 110

"the David" (violin), 78–80

Davis, Randy, 159–60, 173, 189–95

Dean, James, 161–63

*Death of a Salesman* (Miller), 81–82

Dellaria, Dave, 278

DeLoach, David, 133

district attorney and landlord, 18

Doro, Lynn and Bill, 126–29

Dougherty, Gloria and Victor, 75–76

Dubois, William, 49

Dubrot, Heidi, 25–30

Dudnick, Herb, 30–32, 202–3

earpiece, 171

electronic chroma-key, 156

elephant trainer, 41–42

elevator etiquette, 157

Elliott, Bob, 155–56

El Niño, 145, 147–48

e-mail as source of stories, 250

emergency dispatcher—Heimlich
   maneuver, 64–65

Emmy Award panel, 153

endings. *see* closings

Farkas, Ray, 45–46, 48

fashion models in furs during
   summer, 144–45

feature stories, 78

Federal Aviation Administration
  (FAA), 66–68
Fine Arts Museums of San Francisco,
  78–80
fires
  fire-fighting plane collision, 168–69
  the Fountain Fire (northern Calif.),
    125–29
  Interstate 80 forest fire, 221–22
  Oakland Hills firestorm, 224–30
  warehouse fire, 161
first grader's first day, 89–90
follow-up stories, 53
football player, intoxicated, 49
Ford, Richard, 43
forest fire in northern Calif., 125–29
formula for stories, 15
"The Fountain Fire," 127–29
14-year-old entertainment reporter,
  247–48
Fraser, Jack, 133–34
*Fred TV* (webcast), 248
Freedman, Alicia, 92, 283
Freedman, Lauren, 257–58, 276, 283
Freedman, Mike, 92, 106, 283
Freedman, Susan, 283
Freeman, Morgan, 216
Fremont or Little Kabul, 250
Fresno High School Warriors, 210–12
Fuller Brush salesman, 80–82
Fyffe, Bill, 180–82

Galaxy 4, 236–37
General Motors and Toyota, 90–91
Gillibert, Alice, 239–45
Gillibert, Ralph, 238–45
girl with the red ball, 54
glamour, 87–88
goldfish in sewer system, 31–35
golf tournament, Woods and Costner,
  159–60
the Goofball House, 257–59

Gorychev, Sergey, 140
Gramados, Carol, 254–59
Grant, Lily, 162
Grateful Dead hire Latvala, 220
Griffin, John, 239
Griswold, George, 90–91, 111–15
Ground Zero
  "Ground Zero," 272–76
  New York City, 262–64
  overview, 264–66
  writing the story, 271–72
Guerneville, Calif., 187–89
Guintini, Ron, 119–21
gum on the sidewalk, 88–89

Hall, Norman, 80–82
Hanks, Todd, 111–15
Harned, Patrick, 41–42
Hart, John, 218
Hartman, Steve, 218
Hastings, Chuck, 114
"heads-up" attitude, 101
heat wave in San Francisco, 144–49
Heifetz, Jascha, 78
Heimlich instructions during call,
  64–65
Hemingway, Ernest, 221
"High Rents," 26–30
highway closing (snowstorm), 14–15
homelessness in San Francisco,
  111–15
human interest stories, 238–45,
  250–52, 252–59, 257–59
"hybrid" car, 90–91

IFB (Interruptible Feedback Device),
  171
"Indian Summer," 146–49
Interstate 80 forest fire, 221–22
interviews
  of children, 54–57, 90
  of elderly and veterans, 57–60

of police, 180–82, 234–36
of politicians, 49–51
of victims, 52–54
*see also* subjects
interview techniques
accepting "no," 18
camera placement, 45
chameleon theory, 17–18
"c'mon," 48
eye contact, 46
lighting, 44, 45, 124–25, 153
listening, 43–44, 47
microphones, 44–45, 90, 133, 153,
171
positioning subjects, 46, 155
pushing, 19–20, 40, 264
rapport development, 44–45, 47–48,
56–57
selling the idea to subjects, 17–18,
23, 41–43
subject selection, 24–25, 37–40, 57
tact, 51–54, 280
*see also* questions; sound bites; tools
Iraq, 106
*Iron Chef,* 117

Jack's Grill, 75–76
James Dean Memorial, 161–63
Jerris, Rand, 4–6
"Jobless," 20–22
Joey's scrapbook, 74–76
John Paul II, Pope, 201–3
Jones, Charles, 258–59
journalistic formula, 15

Kabasakalis, Johnny, 89–90
KABC-TV, 92, 179–80
Kaufman, Mark, 133
Keeshan, Kevin, 233, 236
kerosene, antimisting, 66–68
key words, 168–69

KGO-TV, 3, 16, 93, 106, 123, 140, 223,
233
Knapp, Don, 174–75
Komodo dragon, 69–70
KRON-TV, 30–32, 52, 90, 111, 175,
201, 217–18
Kuralt, Charles, 47

Lamano, Rose and Bob, 265
landlord and district attorney, 18
Latvala, Dick, 220
Laughlin, Doug, 3–6, 106–8, 170–71
Laursen, John, 53
"The Lawn," 240–45
lawn contest, 238–45
Lentz, Steve, 180–82
*Let's Make a Deal,* 24–25
Letterman, David, 281
lighting, 44, 45, 124–25, 153
Linkletter, Art, 55–56
listening
in interviews, 43–44, 47–48
to your inner voice, 219–22
Little Kabul, 250
live shots
anchors and, 66, 174–76
guidelines for, 168–76
live shot inserts, 172–73
location references, 170
overview, 165–68
package scripts and talk-backs,
173–74
personal horror story, 176–77
speaking in, 168–69, 171
transitions and, 174
wrapped around packages, 14
*see also* stand-ups
Liz Taylor and the Pope, 201–3
local knowledge, 106–7, 109–10
luck, 106
Lukaszewski, Leon, 124–25
Luttrell, Helen, 251–52

Lyon, Greg, 217–18

Macy's and Candlestick Park, 201–3
Magee, Bill, 238
Major, Devorah, 220
major league feud in a minor league
    setting, 250–52
the math wiz, 15–16
McGee, Kerry, 209–10
McRoskey Airflex Co., 237
Medill, Fred and Carey, 247–48
Memorial Day lunch, 74–76
*Me 'n Henry* (Swan), 278–81
metaphors, 106, 208–9, 220
"The Metro," 141–43
microphones, 44–45, 90, 133, 153, 171
Middletown, Calif., 189–95
"Middletown Spelling," 191–95
Miller, Arthur, 81–82
Milligan, Dennis, 145
mining for details, 119, 234–36
minor league baseball and swearing
    rights, 250–52
Mortensen, Chris, 220–21
Moscow subway system, 139–43
motivation, 111, 234, 280

NASA, 66–68
national anthem tryouts, 230–31
national lawn contest, 238–45
NBC News, 218
*NBC News Overnight,* 30
Negron, Elliott, 235–36
news. *see entries beginning with*
    *"television news"*
newsboy, 247–48
newspapers, 22, 189, 250–51
New York City, 262–64
    *see also* Ground Zero
ninetieth homicide victim, 219
nonhuman subjects, 30, 88, 215
Norcross, Brian, 176–77

the "no-swear" lady, 250–52
Nova and Corolla as one, 90–91

Oakland Hills firestorm, 224–30
Oakland Raiders parking lot, 131–34
objective and subjective, 40
Olympic Club (San Francisco), 106–8
the One Book Bookstore, 278–81
"On the Street: Lost and Forgotten,"
    111–15
openings
    details and, 120
    examples, 15, 157, 168
    Grateful Dead hire Latvala, 220
    humanizing with, 118
    live shot inserts, 172–73
    match to the story, 214
    structure and, 64, 65, 70, 71, 73, 76
opposites, using, 139–49
Ortega, Deborah, 266–69

Paccini, Gary, 223–24, 229
packages
    live shot wrapped around, 14
    scripts for, 173–74
    structure of, 74–76, 125–27, 170–73
    suitcase theory of, 183–86
    timelines and, 66
Padmore, Demetrius, 264
Partee, Pam, 17, 72–74, 253
Pele the (burned) cat, 228–29
Pelosi, Nancy, 50–51
Peninsula Ford, 235–36
Pera, Dave, 100
perfection, 130
perspectives
    bad side/good side, 187–89
    of children, 90
    lighting and camera angles, 124–25
    nonhuman, 30–35, 88
    outside the frame, 118–21

scene variations, 121–23, 134, 161, 170–71
of subjects, 43–44
television viewers', 184–86, 201–3, 238, 245, 249
*see also* story types; timelines
photographers, working with
lighting stand-ups, 153
mobile cameras, 170
panning by, 180–82
stress and tension, 44
subject/shot priority, 46
as a team, 111–15, 209–10, 217
Picci, Carla, 122–23
plastics company explosion, 119–22
politicians
Baldwin, Steve, 191–95
Clinton, 106–9, 248
overview, 49–51, 200–203
Polling, Chuck, 31–35
polliwog water, 278–79
Port of Oakland, 15–16
potato chip watcher, 118
Powell, Clyde, 125–27, 161–63
press vs. photo passes, 3–4, 6
Price, Howard, 263
production techniques, 20–22, 172
profiles, 78

questions, asking
overview, 37–38, 96, 111, 113–14, 248, 252–53
the right people, 17, 25, 234–35
the right question(s), 18, 42–44, 49, 51, 56, 59–60, 157, 194, 269
the right way, 45–48, 50–51, 60–61, 264
"Why?" 40, 258–59
questions, not asking, 51–54
questions, timing of, 47–48

Raider Nation, 131–34

rapport development, 44–45, 47, 56–57
Reboul, Claude, 258–59
Redford, Robert, 216
the red house, 257–59
religion, 200–203
rental prices (San Francisco), 22–30
reporters. *see* television news reporters
Revolution Square (Moscow), 139–43
Richmond (Calif.) explosion, 119–22, 120–21
"riding the elephant," 41
Ripkin, Cal, Jr., 99–106
*A River Runs Through It* (movie), 216
Rockwell, Nyal "Rocky," 72–74, 78
rookie baseball league—bubble gum, 222
Roosevelt, Franklin Delano, 39
Rowland, Ken, 177
Rubidub (homeless man), 112–15
rules and theories
be a reporter, 154
chameleon theory, 17–18
failure is not an option, 261
report what you find, 187–89
rule of threes, 214–15
suitcase theory of packaging, 183–86
theory of opposites, 144–45
write the way you speak, 206
*see also* tools

Salcido murders, 52–54
Sanders, Rick, 132
San Francisco Giants, 48
San Francisco's annual cable-car bell-ringing championships, 71–72
Santana High School shooting, 214–15
Saxton, Herb, 101
school shooting, Santana High, 214–15
Schwarzenegger, Arnold, 49–50

scripts. *see* story scripts
"see what you can find" stories,
  263–64
September 11, 208–9
  *see also* Ground Zero
sewer blows up (San Francisco), 172
*The Shawshank Redemption,* 216
Sistine Chapel of grass, 239
snowstorm closes highway, 14–15
sound bites
  background noise, 44, 213
  bridges and, 154, 158, 213
  editing, 212
  keeping fresh, 46–47
  opening and closing with, 77, 172
  overview, 38–40, 209–12
  practicing for, 216
  transitions and, 159, 210–12,
    240–45, 254–59
Spear, Peter, 175–76
spelling in Middletown, Calif., 189–95
spin control, 50, 238
*The Sportswriter* (Ford), 43
stage fright, 42, 168
stand-ups
  as added value, 243, 270
  ad-libbing, 159–60, 161–63, 168–69
  as bridges, 154, 158, 213
  earpiece, 171
  microphone and lighting, 153
  overview, 152–53
  transitions and, 158–59, 174
  visual aids, 156–57, 161
  walking and talking, 155–56, 162–63
  *see also* live shots
Stanley the cat, 215
state trooper at auto accident, 40
statues, Revolution Square (Moscow),
  139–43
Steigler, Franz, 58, 59, 60–61
stolen car ring, 233–36
Stolpa, Jim and Jennifer, 51–52

*Stories from the Heartland*
  at Ground Zero, 264–66
  "Ground Zero," the story, 271–76
  New York City, 262–64
  Ortega and Glesta, 266–70
  overview, 261
  teddy bears, 267, 270
story development techniques
  bubble gum practice, 88–89
  counterpoint, 139–49
  finding an unusual angle, 101–3,
    239–40, 272–76
  the formula, 15
  gaining entrance, 7–8, 96, 107
  humanizing your subjects, 40, 118
  keeping it simple, 183–84, 200–203,
    207–8, 217–19
  leading viewers into the story, 71–74
  mining for details, 119, 234–36
  overview, 82–83
  production techniques, 20–22, 172
  scene sets as narrative, 69–71
  survival skills, 8–9
  telling the truth, 15, 187–89, 223–31
  *see also* interview techniques; tools;
    writing
story scripts
  "Cal Ripkin's Last Game in
    Oakland," 103–6
  "Claire the Goldfish," 32–35
  "Clinton in the Woods," 108–9
  "Crash, Bang, 'Go Raiders!'" 134–37
  "The Fountain Fire," 127–29
  "Ground Zero," 272–76
  "High Rents," 26–30
  "Indian Summer," 146–49
  "Jobless," 20–22
  "The Lawn," 240–45
  "The Metro," 141–43
  "Middletown Spelling," 191–95
  "Strangers," 254–57
  "Things to Remember," 225–30

"Tiger's Trophy," 9–12
"0-31," 210–12
story scripts, partial
  cable-car bell-ringing
    championships, 71–72
  Carvers, Nev., 158
  Chambers, Ariz., 73–74
  clemency hearing for convicted
    murderer, 173
  elevator etiquette, 157
  emergency dispatcher, 64–65
  fire-fighting plane collision, 168–69
  golf tournament, Woods and
    Costner, 159–60
  gum on the sidewalk, 88–89
  Interstate 80 forest fire, 222
  James Dean Memorial, 162–63
  jet crash, 68
  Memorial Day, 76
  national anthem tryouts, 231
  ninetieth homicide victim, 219
  plastics company explosion, 120–21
  potato chip watcher, 118
  rookie baseball league—bubble gum,
    222
  Santana High School shooting,
    214–15
  searching the dump, 71
  Stanley the cat, 215
  warehouse fire, 161
  World's Newest Oldest Human, 221
story structure
  choosing, 66, 271–72
  pacing stories, 209–12
  of packages, 74–76, 125–27, 170–73
  voiceovers, 125, 172
  see also closings; openings; timelines;
    writing
story types
  character studies/human interest,
    238–45, 250–52, 252–59, 257–59
  daily news, 14, 22, 39

features, 78
follow-ups, 53
overview, 66, 122
profiles, 78
"see what you can find," 263–64
think piece, 223–30
threads, 6–7, 131–37, 236
see also live shots; packages; stand-
  ups
"Strangers," 254–59
structure. see story structure
subjective and objective, 40
subjects
  animals as, 30–35, 215, 228–29
  humanizing, 40, 118
  listening to speech patterns, 47–48
  overview, 14–16, 18–22, 26–35,
    238–45
  perspective of, 43–44
  positioning, 46, 155
  selecting, 24–25, 37–40, 57
  selling the idea to, 17–18, 23, 41–43
  see also interviews
Sudweeks, James, 213
suitcase theory of packaging, 183–86
survival skills, 8–9
Swan, Walter and Deloris, 278–81
swearing rights and baseball, 250–52

tact, 51–54, 280
tactile and visual cues, 60
tags, 170–71, 172
  see also closings
talk-backs, 173–74
Taylor, Elizabeth, 201–3
teddy bears, 267, 270
telephone game, 238
television news crew challenges
  anchor tells all while introducing live
    shot, 174–76
  assignment expands late in the day,
    125–27

feed doesn't go through, 173–74
finding stories, 145, 249–52, 262, 272–76
getting past the front line, 7–8, 107
press vs. photo passes, 3–4, 6
schedule mishaps, 90–91
unruly teenagers, 177
television news reporters, in general
acrobats compared to, 261
anchors and, 66, 174–76
changing the world, 277, 281
chronic traits, 95
fishermen compared to, 106
"heads-up" attitude, 101
inquisitive nature of, 252–53
news dialect, 206
photographers, working with, 44, 46, 153, 170, 180–82, 209–10, 217
qualifications, 91–93, 96–97, 106, 280
see also live shots; stand-ups
television news reporting as a career
data maintenance, 110
immersion in the job, 94, 110–11
personal story, 91–93
pleasing managers, 95
survival of the fit, 93–94
wannabes, 129–30, 151–52, 171, 184–86, 216
telling the truth, 15, 187–89, 223–31
Terminator II, 49–50
theories. see rules and theories
theory of opposites, 144–45
"Things to Remember," 224–30
think pieces, 223–30
35 feet of honesty, 45
Thorpe, Mabel, 118
threads, 6–7, 131–37, 236
three ways to sound consistent, 171
"Tiger's Trophy," 9–12
time, relentless march of, 3
timelines

expanding the time frame, 122–23
managing, 96
overview, 63, 66–68, 68–69
structure of, 66
see also closings; openings; story scripts
timing, 47–48, 209–12
Tkachenko, Maxim, 140
tools
"c'mon," 48
journalistic formula, 15
live shot guidelines, 168–76
local knowledge, 106–7, 109–10
luck, 106
for rapport development, 44–45, 47, 56–57
rule of threes, 214–15
selecting subjects, 24–25
shading objective with subjective, 40
survival techniques, 8–9
tact, 51–54, 280
three ways to sound consistent, 171
visual and tactile cues, 60
writing practice, 216
see also interview techniques; rules and theories; story development techniques
Torres, Anthony, 264
Toyota and General Motors, 90–91
train "derailment" in Louisville, Ky., 176–77
Transamerica Pyramid (San Francisco), 157
transitions
from anchors, 66, 174–76
live shots and, 174
sound bites and, 159, 212–13, 240–45, 254–59
stand-ups and, 158–59, 174
Trash Bag Murderer, 180–82
Trexler, Elsa, 93
Tringali, Carmelo, 7–8

trouble. *see* television news crew
   challenges
truth, telling the, 15, 187–89, 223–31
TV news. *see entries beginning with*
   *"television news"*

unemployment line, 16–22
UN weapons inspection (Iraq)
   resolution, 106
U.S. Open trophy, 3–6, 7–12
Utsler, Max, 40

vandals in Middletown, Calif., 189–95
visual aids, 60, 156–57, 161
voiceovers, 125, 172

WABC-TV, 263
wannabes, 129–30, 151–52, 171,
   184–86, 216
warehouse fire, 161
Watkowski, Tracey, 107
WAVE-TV, 209
Webster, Martha, 189–95
Weiss, Milt, 223
Williams, McKinley, 219
Willy Loman *(Death of a Salesman),*
   81–82
wireless communications and Galaxy
   4, 236–37
WLKY-TV, 176–77
Wong, Stan, 221–22
Woods, Tiger, 9, 159–60
World Series 2002, 48

"World's Newest Oldest Human,"
   220–21
World War II, 57–61
writing
   active verbs, 207
   "Benihana trap," 200
   creativity and, 63–68, 70, 73–74,
      119–20
   determining start and finish, 74–76
   experience the story, 96, 219,
      221–22, 224–25, 245
   fitting it all in, 96, 122, 271–72
   keep it simple, 183–84, 200–203,
      207–8, 217–19
   maintain a rhythm, 214–15
   metaphors, 106, 208–9, 220
   news dialect, 206
   overview, 205–6
   practicing, 88–89, 216
   relaxed clarity, 220–21
   as a team member, 111–15, 209–10
   telling the truth, 15, 187–89, 223–31
   *see also* closings; openings;
      perspectives; story development
      techniques
*Writing Broadcast News—Shorter,*
   *Sharper, Stronger* (Block), 209
writing practice, 216

Yee, Leetha, 167
Yuba City, Calif., 123

"0-31," 210–12